Children's
Illustrated
THESAURUS

Children's Illustrated THESAURUS

Written by **Sue Graves**

Illustrated by **Tim Hutchinson**

PaRragon

Bath New York Singapore Hong Kong Cologne Delhi Melbourne

Designer: Fiona Grant

This edition published 2009 for Index Books Ltd

Parragon
Queen Street House
4 Queen Street
Bath BA1 1HE, UK

ISBN 978-1-4054-8761-0

Printed in China

Contents

Introduction

What is a thesaurus?

A **thesaurus** is similar to a dictionary. But instead of just giving you the meaning of the word you have looked up, as a dictionary does, a thesaurus gives you a list of other words with similar meanings (*synonyms*). Sometimes a thesaurus also gives you words with opposite meanings (*antonyms*).

A thesaurus is a very useful book. It can increase your written and spoken vocabulary and help you use more interesting words when you write!

Alphabet band
For each letter of the alphabet there is a different coloured band across the top of the page.

Alphabet letter
The letters inside the circle tell you that all the words on this page begin with the letter **b**.

Header word
The word at the top of the left-hand page shows you the first headword that appears on the page. The word at the top of the right-hand page shows you the last headword that appears on the page.

Headword
The headword is the main word that you look up to find synonyms for it. The headwords appear in alphabetical order.

Feature headword
For this headword there are several related words with illustrations that are linked to, but do not mean exactly the same as, the headword. These words will help you develop your writing.

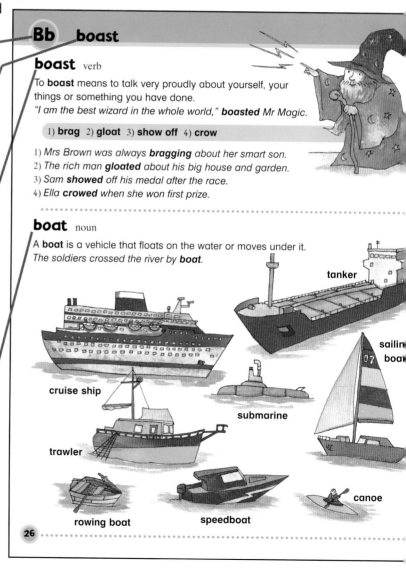

Bb **boast**

boast verb
To **boast** means to talk very proudly about yourself, your things or something you have done.
"I am the best wizard in the whole world," **boasted** *Mr Magic.*

1) **brag** 2) **gloat** 3) **show off** 4) **crow**

1) *Mrs Brown was always* **bragging** *about her smart son.*
2) *The rich man* **gloated** *about his big house and garden.*
3) *Sam* **showed** off *his medal after the race.*
4) *Ella* **crowed** *when she won first prize.*

boat noun
A **boat** is a vehicle that floats on the water or moves under it.
The soldiers crossed the river by **boat**.

tanker

cruise ship

submarine

sailin
boa

trawler

rowing boat

speedboat

canoe

26

How to use this thesaurus

Like a dictionary, words are listed alphabetically in a thesaurus. The word you look up first of all is the headword. After the headword, you can find out what part of speech the word is and what it means. You will also find a sentence showing you how to use the word.

Next, you will find a list of synonyms. These are followed by sentences that show how you might use the synonyms in your writing. If the headword has antonyms (*opposites*), these are listed last of all.

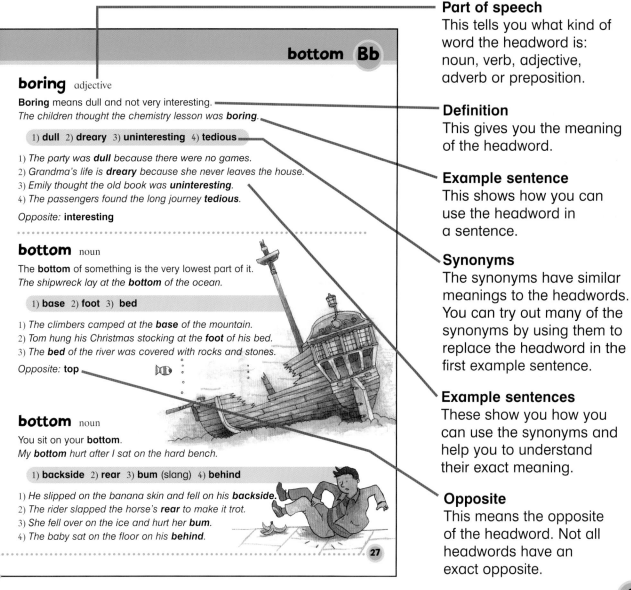

bottom Bb

boring   adjective

Boring means dull and not very interesting.
*The children thought the chemistry lesson was **boring**.*

> 1) **dull**   2) **dreary**   3) **uninteresting**   4) **tedious**

1) *The party was **dull** because there were no games.*
2) *Grandma's life is **dreary** because she never leaves the house.*
3) *Emily thought the old book was **uninteresting**.*
4) *The passengers found the long journey **tedious**.*

Opposite: **interesting**

bottom   noun

The **bottom** of something is the very lowest part of it.
*The shipwreck lay at the **bottom** of the ocean.*

> 1) **base**   2) **foot**   3) **bed**

1) *The climbers camped at the **base** of the mountain.*
2) *Tom hung his Christmas stocking at the **foot** of his bed.*
3) *The **bed** of the river was covered with rocks and stones.*

Opposite: **top**

bottom   noun

You sit on your **bottom**.
*My **bottom** hurt after I sat on the hard bench.*

> 1) **backside**   2) **rear**   3) **bum** (slang)   4) **behind**

1) *He slipped on the banana skin and fell on his **backside**.*
2) *The rider slapped the horse's **rear** to make it trot.*
3) *She fell over on the ice and hurt her **bum**.*
4) *The baby sat on the floor on his **behind**.*

27

Part of speech
This tells you what kind of word the headword is: noun, verb, adjective, adverb or preposition.

Definition
This gives you the meaning of the headword.

Example sentence
This shows how you can use the headword in a sentence.

Synonyms
The synonyms have similar meanings to the headwords. You can try out many of the synonyms by using them to replace the headword in the first example sentence.

Example sentences
These show you how you can use the synonyms and help you to understand their exact meaning.

Opposite
This means the opposite of the headword. Not all headwords have an exact opposite.

able adjective

If you are **able** to do something, you can do it.
*The magician was **able** to do card tricks.*

> 1) **capable** 2) **skilful**

1) *She was **capable** of writing neatly when she tried.*
2) *Jenny was a **skilful** basketball player.*

Opposites: **incapable, unable**

about adverb

About means almost or nearly.
*Jim had **about** four more maths questions to finish.*

> 1) **almost** 2) **approximately** 3) **nearly** 4) **roughly**

1) *It was **almost** time for dinner.*
2) *The bus was **approximately** five minutes late.*
3) *There were **nearly** 20 children at Jack's party.*
4) ***Roughly** seven children stayed home from school today.*

above preposition

Something that is **above** is higher up.
*The plane flew **above** the clouds.*

> 1) **over** 2) **on top of** 3) **upon**

1) *The walkers climbed **over** the hill to reach the other side.*
2) *The window cleaner stood **on top of** the ladder.*
3) *Mum put seven candles **upon** the birthday cake.*

Opposites: **below, under**

absent adjective

If you are **absent** from something, you are away from it.
*Andrew was **absent** because he had chicken pox.*

> 1) **away** 2) **gone** 3) **missing**

1) *The Jones family was **away** for the holidays.*
2) *There were lots of cakes, but suddenly they were **gone**!*
3) *Grandma was worried because her pet cat was **missing**.*

Opposite: **present**

accident noun

An **accident** is something bad that happens by chance.
*Sam had an **accident** on his bike.*

> 1) **disaster** 2) **crash** 3) **collision**

1) *It was a **disaster** when the school burned down.*
2) *Two big tankers were involved in the **crash**.*
3) *The **collision** took place on an icy road.*

active adjective

An **active** person or animal moves around a lot.
*Our new puppy is very **active**.*

> 1) **lively** 2) **energetic** 3) **vigorous**

1) *The **lively** children ran around the playground.*
2) *The circus acrobats were very **energetic**.*
3) *The boys played a **vigorous** game of football.*

actor noun

An **actor** is someone who performs in a film or a play.
*The **actor** stood in the middle of the stage.*

> 1) **player** 2) **performer** 3) **star**

1) *The three **players** bowed in front of the audience.*
2) *The street **performer** made everyone laugh.*
3) *The **star** of the film wore a beautiful dress.*

add verb

You **add** numbers together to find their total.
*You can use a calculator to **add** a list of numbers.*

> 1) **count** 2) **total**

1) *My little brother can **count** up to 100.*
2) *The shopkeeper had to **total** the day's takings.*

Opposite: **subtract**

admire verb

To **admire** means to like and respect something or someone.
*The people went to the museum to **admire** the paintings.*

> 1) **adore** 2) **praise** 3) **worship**

1) *"I **adore** pop music," said Donna.*
2) *The teacher **praised** the children's good work.*
3) *She **worshipped** her older brother and his friends.*

admit verb

To **admit** is to accept that something is true.
*The thief had to **admit** that he had stolen the money.*

> 1) **accept** 2) **own up** 3) **confess** 4) **acknowledge**

1) *Ben cannot **accept** that he is no longer in the football team.*
2) *He **owned up** to breaking the window.*
3) *I told my brother to **confess** the truth.*
4) *She **acknowledged** that her dog had eaten the food.*

Opposite: **deny**

adult adjective

Adult means grown up or developed.
*Every child had to be accompanied by an **adult** person.*

> 1) **fully grown** 2) **grown-up** 3) **mature**

1) *Most cats are **fully grown** by the time they are two years old.*
2) *The swimmers were accompanied by two **grown-up** lifeguards.*
3) *The girls in the sixth form behave in a **mature** way.*

afraid adjective

If you are **afraid**, you are scared or frightened.
*The little girl was **afraid** of the dark.*

> 1) **scared** 2) **fearful** 3) **frightened** 4) **terrified**

1) *Our kitten is **scared** of loud noises.*
2) *The **fearful** knight ran away from the battle.*
3) *The puppy was **frightened** by the big dog.*
4) *The old man was **terrified** of ghosts.*

Opposites: **confident, unafraid**

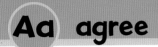

Aa agree

agree verb

If you **agree** with someone, you think the same as that person.
*Everyone **agreed** that the new building was ugly!*

> 1) **get along** 2) **concur** 3) **accept** 4) **side with**

1) *Ben **gets along** well with his stepbrother.*
2) *The teacher **concurred** that the maths question was difficult.*
3) *The doctor **accepted** that his patient was sick.*
4) *Lucy always **sides with** Mark during an argument.*

Opposite: **disagree**

aircraft noun

An **aircraft** is a machine that flies through the air.
*A helicopter is a kind of **aircraft**.*

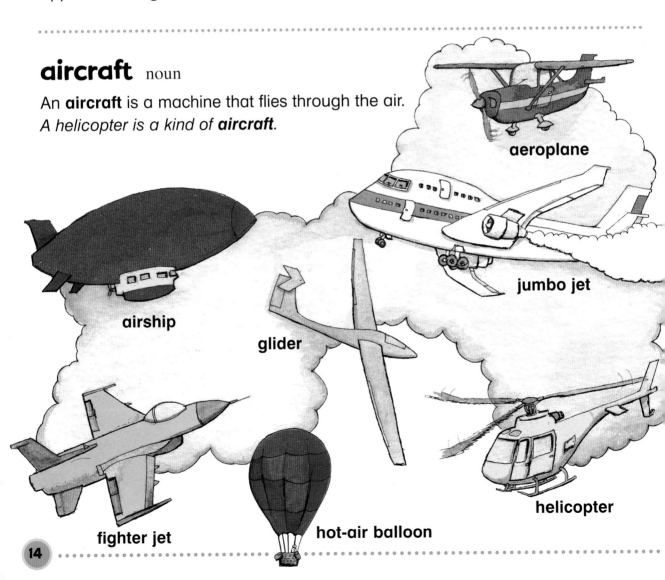

aeroplane

jumbo jet

airship

glider

helicopter

fighter jet

hot-air balloon

alert adjective

If you are **alert**, you are ready for action.
*The security guard was **alert** as he opened the door.*

> 1) **attentive** 2) **observant** 3) **watchful** 4) **sharp**

1) *Jack is **attentive** and always listens carefully to his teacher.*
2) *The burglar was spotted by an **observant** police officer.*
3) *The soldiers were **watchful** in case the enemy attacked.*
4) *The **sharp** girl spotted the missing jewel.*

amusing adjective

Something that is **amusing** is funny and makes people laugh.
*Mark's uncle told an **amusing** story about his dog.*

> 1) **enjoyable** 2) **funny** 3) **hilarious**

1) *Everyone had an **enjoyable** time at the show.*
2) *The girls watched a **funny** cartoon on TV.*
3) *The circus clowns were really **hilarious**.*

Opposites: **boring, dull**

angry adjective

Angry means cross or annoyed.
*Mum was **angry** when the dog ate her lunch.*

> 1) **annoyed** 2) **cross** 3) **displeased** 4) **furious**

1) *We were **annoyed** because the bus was late.*
2) *Grandad gets **cross** when he loses his glasses.*
3) *The teacher was **displeased** with the noisy class.*
4) *Mary was **furious** when her brother took her sweets.*

animal noun

An **animal** is a living creature that breathes and moves around.
*There are lots of **animals** in the jungle.*

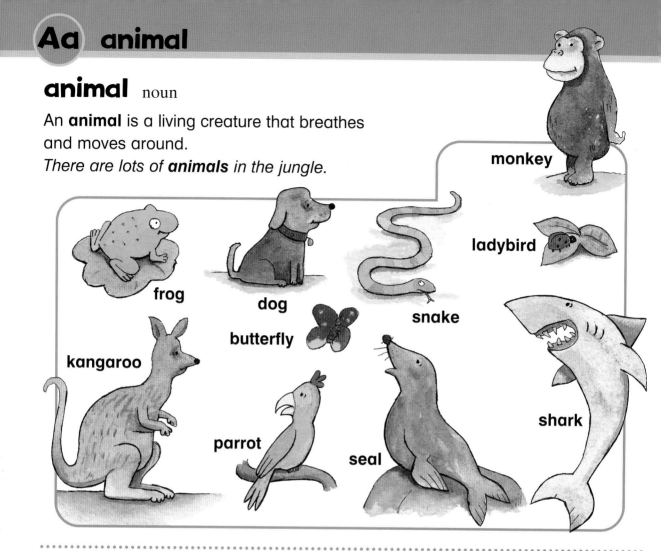

monkey

ladybird

frog

dog

snake

butterfly

kangaroo

parrot

seal

shark

annoy verb

If you **annoy** people, you irritate them.
*Joe liked to **annoy** his big sister.*

1) **bother** 2) **irritate** 3) **pester** 4) **tease**

1) *"Don't **bother** me now," said Mum, reading the newspaper.*
2) *The rash on my arm started to **irritate** me.*
3) *The twins always **pester** their mum when they go shopping.*
4) *I **tease** my best friend about her purple hair!*

Opposite: **please**

answer verb

When you **answer**, you say or write something to someone who asks a question.
*"How old are you?" asked the man. "I'm seven," **answered** Katie.*

> 1) **reply** 2) **respond** 3) **retort**

1) *The thief **replies** quickly to the police officer's question.*
2) *The waiter **responded** to our complaint about the food.*
3) *"That's such an awful headline!" **retorted** the journalist.*

appear verb

If something **appears**, it moves to a place where you can see it.
*The ghost suddenly **appeared** in the doorway.*

> 1) **come into view** 2) **come to light** 3) **loom** 4) **turn up**

1) *The ship **came into view** over the horizon.*
2) *The missing documents **came to light** after a search.*
3) *A sinister figure **loomed** out of the fog.*
4) *Michael was sure his missing trainers would **turn up**.*

Opposite: **disappear**

argue verb

If you **argue** with someone, you do not agree with that person.
*The boys **argue** about which football team is the best.*

> 1) **bicker** 2) **disagree** 3) **quarrel** 4) **squabble**

1) *The sisters **bicker** about whose turn it is to ride the pony.*
2) *My mum and dad **disagree** over silly things.*
3) *When people **quarrel** they often shout at each other.*
4) *Martha and Emily **squabbled** over the remote control for the TV.*

Opposite: **agree**

arrange verb

If you **arrange** something, you work out how to do something and then do it.
*I'm going to **arrange** a surprise party for my sister's birthday.*

> 1) **plan** 2) **prepare** 3) **organize**

1) *It took a long time to **plan** our safari trip.*
2) *The hotel staff **prepared** the conference room.*
3) *He **organized** a meeting between the parents and the teachers.*

ask verb

You **ask** a question in order to find out the answer.
*The children **ask** their teacher lots of questions.*

> 1) **request** 2) **query** 3) **interrogate** 4) **enquire**

1) *The dentist **requested** that I come back in six months.*
2) *The farmer **queried** what the vet said.*
3) *The police officer **interrogated** the suspect.*
4) *Molly **enquired** whether her neighbour was feeling better.*

Opposites: **answer, reply**

asleep adjective

If you are **asleep**, you are not awake.
*The cat is **asleep** in the easy chair.*

> 1) **sleeping** 2) **dozing** 3) **snoozing** 4) **slumbering**

1) *The **sleeping** baby did not make a sound.*
2) *"Shh! The puppy is **dozing!**"*
3) *It is not wise to wake a **snoozing** tiger!*
4) *The **slumbering** giant snored loudly.*

Opposite: **awake**

awake adjective

If you are **awake** you are alert and aware.
*Bill was **awake** all night long because he couldn't sleep.*

> 1) **alert** 2) **conscious** 3) **attentive**

1) *The explorer was **alert** as he travelled through the jungle.*
2) *Daniel was still **conscious** after the car accident.*
3) *We tried to be **attentive** in our new teacher's class.*

Opposite: **asleep**

awful adjective

Something that is **awful** is very bad or unpleasant.
*Hannah thought her new dress was **awful**!*

> 1) **bad** 2) **horrible** 3) **unpleasant** 4) **ugly**

1) *William's **bad** behaviour upset his mum.*
2) *Josh was **horrible** to his sister and made her cry.*
3) *The ice cream had an **unpleasant** taste.*
4) *Litter in the street looks really **ugly**.*

Opposites: **good, nice**

baby noun

A **baby** is a young child or animal.
*The **baby** was only two months old.*

> 1) **newborn** 2) **child** 3) **infant** 4) **toddler**

1) *Mum cuddled her **newborn** in her arms.*
2) *The **child** had a short nap every afternoon.*
3) *Meg was the youngest **infant** in the nursery.*
4) *The **toddler** played in the paddling pool.*

Opposite: **adult**

bad adjective

Bad means not good.
*The puppy was **bad** and ate Dad's shoe.*

> 1) **naughty** 2) **wicked** 3) **evil**

1) *Our **naughty** cat climbed up the apple tree.*
2) *Everyone was scared of the **wicked** witch.*
3) *The magician cast an **evil** spell.*

Opposite: **good**

bad adjective

If food is **bad**, it is not fit for you to eat.
*Tim ate a **bad** apple and had stomach ache.*

> 1) **rotten** 2) **mouldy** 3) **spoiled** 4) **sour**

1) *The **rotten** apples are lying on the ground.*
2) *Mum put the **mouldy** cheese in the rubbish bin.*
3) *The food was **spoiled** because of the heat.*
4) *No one could drink the **sour** milk.*

bake verb

To **bake** is to cook something in an oven.
*Every Friday, my grandma likes to **bake** cakes.*

> 1) **cook** 2) **heat** 3) **roast**

1) *My dad wears an apron when he **cooks**.*
2) *The chef **heated** the apple pie until it was warm.*
3) *If you **roast** meat slowly it will be tender to eat.*

band noun

A **band** is a number of people who play music together.
*My brother plays the drums in a **band**.*

> 1) **group** 2) **orchestra** 3) **ensemble**

1) *The pop **group** has made a new album.*
2) *There are over 100 musicians in the **orchestra**.*
3) *An **ensemble** played music during the wedding.*

band noun

A **band** is a thin strip of rubber, metal or some other material.
*Tom wore a red **band** on his wrist.*

> 1) **ring** 2) **strap** 3) **strip**

1) *Mary was proud of her diamond **ring**.*
2) *The traveller fastened the **strap** around his suitcase.*
3) *The nurse put a **strip** of bandage over the wound.*

bare adjective

If a part of your body is **bare**, it is not covered with clothing.
*He stood **bare** with his clothes on the floor around him.*

> 1) **naked** 2) **undressed** 3) **nude**

1) *Babies are **naked** when they are born.*
2) *The pirates were **undressed** down to their waists.*
3) *The **nude** statue was on display in the art museum.*

Opposites: **clothed, dressed**

beast noun

A **beast** is a wild animal.
*A tiger is a **beast** that lives in the jungle.*

> 1) **animal** 2) **creature** 3) **monster**

1) *They saw an injured **animal** by the side of the road.*
2) *The **creature** ran into the woods and out of sight.*
3) *People say there is a **monster** in Scotland's Loch Ness.*

beautiful adjective

Beautiful means very pretty.
*The **beautiful** princess wore a dress of green silk.*

> 1) **attractive** 2) **charming** 3) **fine** 4) **lovely**

1) *The **attractive** girl wanted to be a fashion model.*
2) *The little boy had a **charming** smile.*
3) *The shoes were made of **fine** leather.*
4) *There are many **lovely** flowers in the park.*

Opposites: **ugly, unattractive**

behave verb

To **behave** means to act in a certain way.
*The children always **behave** well at their grandma's house.*

> 1) **act** 2) **conduct** 3) **respond**

1) *The guide asked the children to **act** sensibly in the museum.*
2) *You should **conduct** yourself quietly in a church.*
3) *Our puppy **responds** well when you praise her.*

Opposite: **misbehave**

bend verb

If you **bend** something, you make it more curved.
*A strongman can **bend** an iron bar.*

> 1) **twist** 2) **curve** 3) **turn**

1) *Jane **twisted** her long hair into a big knot.*
2) *He **curved** the cardboard around the glass vase.*
3) *The driver **turned** the handle on the truck door.*

Opposite: **straighten**

bend noun

A **bend** is a curve.
*Watch out for the sharp **bend** in the road!*

> 1) **corner** 2) **curve** 3) **turn** 4) **twist**

1) *He drove around the **corner** too fast and crashed the car.*
2) *The designer drew a pattern with lots of **curves** in it.*
3) *The path took a **turn** to the left by the river.*
4) *The speed camera was hidden by a **twist** in the road.*

better adjective

If you feel **better**, you no longer feel ill.
*Ellen was feeling **better** after having mumps.*

> 1) **recovered** 2) **stronger** 3) **fitter** 4) **well**

1) *He felt **recovered** after catching malaria.*
2) *Beth was a lot **stronger** and able to get out of bed.*
3) *The athletes are **fitter** after training hard.*
4) *Now that Sarah is **well** she can start dancing again.*

between preposition

Between means in the middle of.
*The little boy stood **between** his parents.*

> 1) **among** 2) **amid**

1) *The farmer threw the corn **among** the chickens.*
2) *She heard the boy call out **amid** all the noise.*

big adjective

Something that is **big** is large.
*An elephant is a **big** animal.*

> 1) **large** 2) **vast** 3) **immense** 4) **enormous** 5) **huge**

1) *We take a **large** suitcase with us on holiday.*
2) *The Sahara desert is a **vast** area.*
3) *The king and queen lived in an **immense** castle.*
4) *A blue whale is an **enormous** animal.*
5) *The giant had **huge** hands.*

Opposites: **little, small, tiny**

bird noun

A **bird** is an animal with wings and feathers.
*Most **birds** can fly, but an ostrich cannot.*

penguin

owl

blackbird

chicken

ostrich

parrot

duck

swan

bit noun

A **bit** of something is a very small piece.
*She passed me a **bit** of her chocolate bar.*

1) **piece** 2) **chunk** 3) **chip** 4) **fragment**

1) *Mum gave everyone a **piece** of birthday cake.*
2) *He had a **chunk** of cheese and some bread for lunch.*
3) *The carpenter knocked a **chip** of wood out of the table.*
4) *I cut my hand on a tiny **fragment** of glass.*

boast verb

To **boast** means to talk very proudly about yourself, your things, or something you have done.
"I am the best wizard in the whole world," **boasted** *Mr Magic.*

> 1) **brag** 2) **gloat** 3) **show off** 4) **crow**

1) *Mrs Brown was always* **bragging** *about her smart son.*
2) *The rich man* **gloated** *about his big house and garden.*
3) *Sam* **showed off** *his medal after the race.*
4) *Ella* **crowed** *when she won first prize.*

boat noun

A **boat** is a vehicle that floats on the water or moves under it.
The soldiers crossed the river by **boat.**

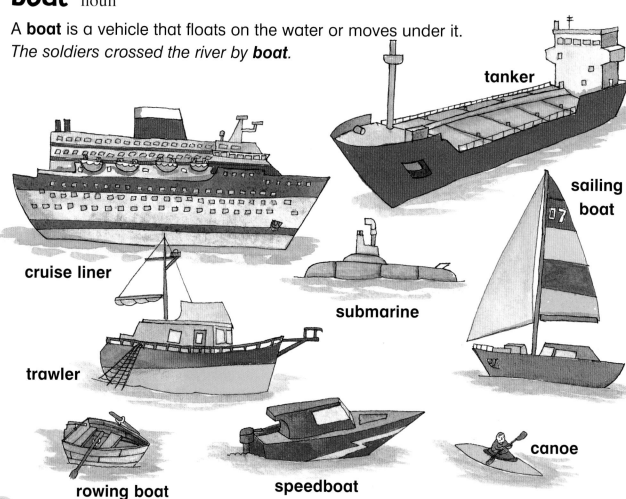

tanker

sailing boat

cruise liner

submarine

trawler

rowing boat

speedboat

canoe

boring adjective

Boring means dull and not very interesting.
*The children thought the chemistry lesson was **boring**.*

> 1) **dull** 2) **dreary** 3) **uninteresting** 4) **tedious**

1) *The party was **dull** because there were no games.*
2) *Grandma's life is **dreary** because she never leaves the house.*
3) *Emily thought the old book was **uninteresting**.*
4) *The passengers found the long journey **tedious**.*

Opposite: **interesting**

bottom noun

The **bottom** of something is the very lowest part of it.
*The shipwreck lay at the **bottom** of the ocean.*

> 1) **base** 2) **foot** 3) **bed**

1) *The climbers camped at the **base** of the mountain.*
2) *Tom hung his Christmas stocking at the **foot** of his bed.*
3) *The **bed** of the river was covered with rocks and stones.*

Opposite: **top**

bottom noun

You sit on your **bottom**.
*My **bottom** hurt after I sat on the hard bench.*

> 1) **backside** 2) **rear** 3) **bum** (slang) 4) **behind**

1) *He slipped on the banana skin and fell on his **backside**.*
2) *The rider slapped the horse's **rear** to make it trot.*
3) *She fell over on the ice and hurt her **bum**.*
4) *The baby sat on the floor on his **behind**.*

brave adjective

If you are **brave**, you are not afraid to do something.
*The **brave** girl dived into the swimming pool.*

1) **bold** 2) **fearless** 3) **daring** 4) **plucky**

1) *The **bold** knight rescued the princess from the tower.*
2) *Tom was **fearless** when he climbed the high wall.*
3) *Only Peter was **daring** enough to jump in the water.*
4) *Mum was very **plucky** to tackle the burglar.*

Opposites: **afraid, scared, timid**

break verb

If you **break** something, you smash it to pieces.
*If you drop a glass on a hard floor, it will usually **break**.*

1) **crack** 2) **shatter** 3) **fracture** 4) **snap**

1) *The storm was so strong that it **cracked** the ship's mast.*
2) *The falling brick **shattered** the window.*
3) *If you **fracture** your leg you will probably have it put in a cast.*
4) *The boy hit the ball so hard that he **snapped** his bat.*

Opposites: **fix, mend, repair**

break noun

A **break** is a short rest or a change in something.
*We got out of the car for a short **break**.*

1) **rest** 2) **pause** 3) **intermission** 4) **gap**

1) *The athlete needed a **rest** after the long race.*
2) *The man took a **pause** from digging in his garden.*
3) *In the play's **intermission** we talked in the lobby.*
4) *The fox squeezed through a **gap** in the fence.*

bright adjective

Something that is **bright** is shiny and gives off light.
*The lights on the Christmas tree were very **bright**.*

> 1) **shiny** 2) **dazzling** 3) **brilliant** 4) **glaring**

1) *I found a **shiny** coin in the street today.*
2) *The stars were **dazzling** in the night sky.*
3) *The **brilliant** diamond sparkled in the light.*
4) *Sunglasses protect your eyes from **glaring** sunlight.*

Opposites: **dim, dull**

bright adjective

A **bright** person is smart and quick to learn.
*Penny was a very **bright** student.*

> 1) **brainy** 2) **smart** 3) **intelligent** 4) **clever**

1) *Bob was so **brainy** that he passed all his tests.*
2) *The **smart** boy thought of a good plan.*
3) *The **intelligent** woman liked doing difficult crossword puzzles.*
4) *The **clever** dog could open the door with his teeth.*

bring verb

If you **bring** something, you carry it with you.
*I will **bring** your present to the birthday party.*

> 1) **carry** 2) **take** 3) **fetch**

1) *The porter **carried** her suitcase onto the train.*
2) *We had to **take** a picnic lunch on the school trip.*
3) *Dad told the dog to **fetch** his slippers.*

build verb

If you **build** something you make it or put it together.
*Grandpa likes to **build** model railways.*

> 1) **make** 2) **assemble** 3) **construct**

1) *Dad is going to **make** a treehouse for us.*
2) *He tried to **assemble** the bookcase by following the instructions.*
3) *The builders **constructed** the new shed very quickly.*

Opposites: **demolish, destroy, knock down**

building noun

A **building** is a place with a roof and walls where you can live,
work, or worship.
*A skyscraper is a very tall **building**.*

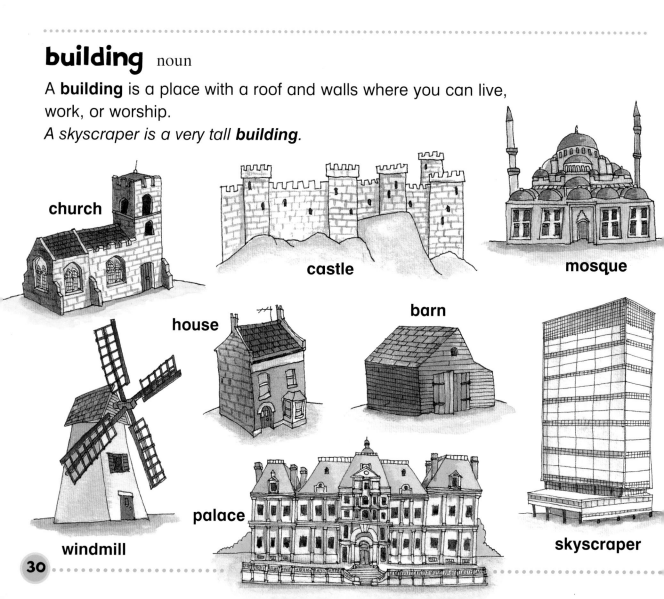

church

castle

mosque

house

barn

windmill

palace

skyscraper

burn verb

If something **burns**, it catches fire and gives off flames.
*The fire **burns** brightly and warms up the campers.*

> 1) **blaze** 2) **flame** 3) **flare**

1) *The fires **blazed** across the forest.*
2) *A match will **flame** briefly and then go out.*
3) *When Mum fanned the fire, the flames
   flared up.*

bury verb

If you **bury** something you place it under the ground.
*Our dog likes to **bury** his bones in the backyard.*

> 1) **conceal** 2) **cover** 3) **hide**

1) *The pirates wanted to **conceal** their treasure in the cave.*
2) *The desert sand has **covered** the ruins of the ancient city.*
3) *Squirrels **hide** their acorns inside tree trunks.*

busy adjective

If you are **busy**, you have lots to do.
*She was having a **busy** day cleaning the house.*

> 1) **active** 2) **occupied** 3) **bustling**

1) *The children spent an **active** day swimming and climbing.*
2) *My brother was **occupied** all day in his bedroom.*
3) *The head teacher is always **bustling** around her office.*

Opposites: **idle, inactive**

call verb

If you **call**, you shout out for someone.
*"I will **call** your names one at a time," said the teacher.*

> 1) **announce** 2) **cry** 3) **yell** 4) **shout**

1) *The referee **announced** the names of the winning teams.*
2) *"Come back here!" **cried** the dog trainer.*
3) *The coach **yelled** to the players on the field.*
4) *Tom was told not to **shout** in class.*

call verb

If you **call** on someone, you visit that person.
*"**Call** when you're walking past," said the old woman.*

> 1) **visit** 2) **come over** 3) **drop by**

1) *I **visit** my grandma every weekend.*
2) *"Can you **come over** to my house to play?" asked Billy.*
3) *The doctor said he would **drop by** on his way home.*

calm adjective

Calm means quiet and not worried or excited.
*"Stay **calm** while I remove the splinter," said Mum.*

> 1) **quiet** 2) **still** 3) **peaceful** 4) **serene**

1) *The children played a **quiet** game of cards.*
2) *You could not hear a sound in the **still** night.*
3) *Grandpa enjoyed the **peaceful** surroundings of the park.*
4) *The old soldier had a **serene** expression.*

care verb

If you **care** about something or someone, you think a lot about that person or thing.
*"I really do **care** about you!" Jack's worried mum said to him.*

> 1) **mind** 2) **be concerned** 3) **worry**

1) *"I don't **mind** if it rains," said the gardener.*
2) *The pilot was **concerned** that his plane was damaged.*
3) *We were **worried** when Jake arrived home late.*

careless adjective

You are **careless** if you do something without thinking about what you are doing.
*Raul was **careless** with his maths homework and made lots of mistakes.*

> 1) **thoughtless** 2) **forgetful** 3) **inconsiderate** 4) **messy**

1) *The **thoughtless** professor forgot to mark the student's work.*
2) *Minnie's grandfather is becoming very **forgetful**.*
3) *Tom could be very **inconsiderate** about other people's feelings.*
4) *"Your work is very **messy**, Andrew," said Mr Lucas. "Do it again!"*

Opposites: **careful, considerate, thoughtful**

carry verb

When you **carry** something, you hold it and move it with you.
*The builder had to **carry** a large pile of bricks.*

> 1) **take** 2) **move** 3) **transport**

1) *We must **take** the rubbish to the dump.*
2) *The movers **moved** the furniture into our new house.*
3) *Lorries **transport** goods all over the country.*

catch verb

If you **catch** something, you take hold of it in your hands.
"Catch the ball, Tom!" shouted the coach.

> 1) **arrest** 2) **capture** 3) **trap** 4) **grab**

1) *The police officer set off to **arrest** the thief.*
2) *The zookeeper tried to **capture** the escaped parrot.*
3) *A spider will **trap** flies in its web.*
4) *Jenny's mum told her that it was not polite to **grab**.*

Opposites: **drop, free, miss**

certain adjective

To be **certain** is to be sure about something.
*Josh was running so fast, he was **certain** he would win.*

> 1) **confident** 2) **satisfied** 3) **positive** 4) **sure**

1) *Dan has worked hard and is **confident** that he will pass the test.*
2) *The baker was **satisfied** that he had baked enough cakes.*
3) *Luke was **positive** that he had handed in his homework.*
4) *The driver was **sure** that the bus would arrive on time.*

Opposites: **doubtful, uncertain, unsure**

change verb

When something **changes** it becomes different.
*My older sister **changes** the colour of her hair every month.*

> 1) **alter** 2) **transform** 3) **modify** 4) **vary**

1) *Mum is going to **alter** my new dress because it's too big.*
2) *The decorator **transformed** her bedroom into a princess's palace.*
3) *The general had to **modify** his battle plans.*
4) *Dad likes to **vary** his route to work each week.*

chase *verb*

To **chase** is to run after someone or something.
*Dogs like to **chase** cats.*

> 1) **run after** 2) **hunt** 3) **pursue** 4) **track**

1) *The hungry leopard **ran after** the herd of gazelle.*
2) *Our cat goes out to **hunt** for food at night.*
3) *The shopkeeper **pursued** the man who stole his money.*
4) *The guide **tracked** the elephants by following their footprints.*

chat *verb*

To **chat** is to talk in an easy, casual way.
*Dad likes to **chat** with our next-door neighbours.*

> 1) **talk** 2) **gossip** 3) **converse**

1) *I **talk** to my best friend on the phone every day.*
2) *Lucy told her sister not to **gossip** about other people.*
3) *Mum **converses** with the butcher whenever she goes into the shop.*

cheap *adjective*

If something is **cheap**, it does not cost much money.
*The clothes on sale were very **cheap**.*

> 1) **reasonable** 2) **inexpensive** 3) **reduced** 4) **affordable**

1) *Mum says we can buy the computer game if it's a* **reasonable** *price.*
2) *Jasmine bought an **inexpensive** dress in the sale.*
3) *The shop had some **reduced** items after Christmas.*
4) *The builder was selling some* **affordable** *new houses.*

*Opposites: **costly**, **expensive***

check verb

When you **check** something you make sure it is right.
*The sailor went to **check** that the ropes were fastened tightly.*

> 1) **examine** 2) **inspect** 3) **test** 4) **look over**

1) *He **examined** the used car very carefully.*
2) *The conductor **inspected** our train tickets.*
3) *Dan **tested** the sea to see how warm it was.*
4) *The teacher **looked over** the children's homework every evening.*

child noun

A **child** is a young boy or girl.
*When I was a **child** I liked to sit on Mum's knee.*

> 1) **baby** 2) **infant** 3) **toddler** 4) **youngster**

1) *Our **baby** liked to sleep in his car seat.*
2) *The **infant** was learning to crawl.*
3) *She takes her **toddler** to nursery every morning.*
4) *The **youngster** helped the blind man across the road.*

Opposites: **adult, grown up**

choose verb

To **choose** is to decide which thing you want from a larger number.
*Adam wants to **choose** a new colour for his bedroom walls.*

> 1) **select** 2) **pick** 3) **take** 4) **elect**

1) *The captain was asked to **select** players for her team.*
2) *We **picked** our favourite toys from the catalogue.*
3) *Mum **took** three lamb chops for supper.*
4) *Every few years people **elect** a new prime minister.*

clean adjective

If something is **clean**, it is not dirty.
She hung the clean towels on the line.

> 1) **fresh** 2) **spotless** 3) **washed** 4) **scoured**

1) *The villagers took **fresh** water from the well.*
2) *She made sure the house was **spotless**.*
3) *The **washed** tennis socks look very white.*
4) *The **scoured** saucepans were sparkling.*

Opposites: **dirty, soiled, unclean**

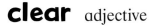

clear adjective

If something is **clear**, you can see through it or into it easily.
The sea was so clear that you could see the bottom.

> 1) **clean** 2) **transparent** 3) **pure** 4) **unclouded**

1) *The **clean** windows sparkled in the sunshine.*
2) *The florist wrapped the flowers in **transparent** paper.*
3) *I like to drink the **pure** water from the spring.*
4) *The water in the mountain stream was **unclouded**.*

Opposite: **cloudy**

clear adjective

Something that is **clear** is easy to understand.
The instructions for making the model castle were clear.

> 1) **plain** 2) **simple** 3) **straightforward** 4) **obvious**

1) *The judge told Jacob to tell the **plain** truth.*
2) *I can only do **simple** maths questions in my head.*
3) *The directions to the museum were **straightforward**.*
4) *Ben finally worked out the **obvious** answer to his question.*

Opposites: **complicated, confusing**

clever adjective

Someone or something that is **clever** is original and imaginative.
*Mark found a **clever** way to store his bicycle.*

> 1) **smart** 2) **ingenious** 3) **quick-witted**

1) *Sam is so **smart** he can name the capital of each country.*
2) *The **ingenious** entertainer made animals out of balloons.*
3) *The fox was **quick-witted** and escaped from the hunters.*

Opposites: **dull, stupid**

climb verb

To **climb** is to go up something.
*The window cleaner **climbs** the ladder to clean the windows.*

> 1) **go up** 2) **ascend** 3) **clamber**

1) *You **go up** a hill to reach our house.*
2) *They took four days to **ascend** Mount Kilimanjaro.*
3) *They **clambered** up the cliff at the back of the beach.*

Opposites: **descend, go down**

close verb

When you **close** something you shut it.
*The passenger was told to **close** the door behind him.*

> 1) **shut** 2) **fasten** 3) **lock** 4) **slam**

1) *Dad **shut** the front door with a bang.*
2) *We **fastened** the windows before leaving the house.*
3) *The security guard **locked** the factory gates.*
4) *The pirate **slammed** the lid of the treasure chest.*

Opposite: **open**

clothes noun

Clothes are the things you wear on your body. Trousers, skirts, shirts and sweaters are different kinds of **clothes**.

My sister keeps her clothes in a big wardrobe.

shorts

suit

trousers

skirt

coat

jacket

dress

T-shirt

jeans

shirt

cold adjective

If something is **cold**, it is not hot.

It was such a cold day that I put on my hat and scarf.

1) **chilly** 2) **icy** 3) **frosty** 4) **freezing**

1) *The sheep stood still in the chilly weather.*
2) *The icy wind blew strongly.*
3) *The children could see their breath in the frosty air.*
4) *Megan was freezing as she walked to school in the snow.*

Opposites: **hot, warm**

Cc collect

collect verb

To **collect** is to bring things together.

*George **collects** all kinds of shells.*

> 1) **save** 2) **assemble** 3) **gather**

1) *We **save** glass bottles so we can recycle them.*
2) *The children had to **assemble** outside during the fire drill.*
3) *Every autumn we **gather** blackberries to make jam.*

colour noun

A **colour** is the way you see something when you look at it in the light.

*There are seven **colours** in a rainbow.*

> 1) **shade** 2) **tint** 3) **hue**

1) *Her dress was a pretty **shade** of blue.*
2) *The painter added a red **tint** to the white paint.*
3) *Mary had hair ribbons of every **hue**.*

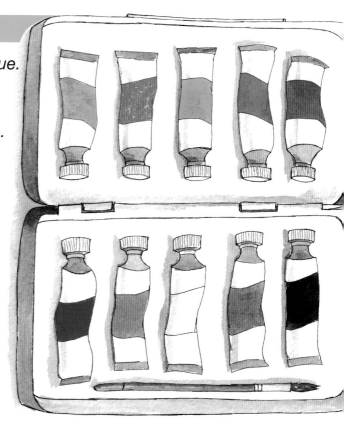

yellow: amber, lemon, gold
orange: coral, tangerine
green: emerald, lime, olive
blue: navy, turquoise
red: crimson, scarlet

purple: lilac, lavender, violet
pink: magenta, rose
white: cream, ivory
brown: beige, chocolate, tan
black: ebony, jet

come verb

To **come** is to move towards someone or something.
*Robert asked everyone to **come** to his party.*

> 1) **appear** 2) **arrive** 3) **approach** 4) **reach**

1) *The magician made the rabbit **appear** out of a hat.*
2) *Our friends will **arrive** at 2 o'clock.*
3) *We **approached** the castle through the main gates.*
4) *We **reached** the station as the train was leaving.*

Opposites: **depart, go, leave**

complete adjective

If something is **complete**, nothing is missing from it.
*My dad has a **complete** set of Shakespeare's plays.*

> 1) **full** 2) **whole** 3) **total** 4) **entire**

1) *Sarah has a **full** set of art brushes.*
2) *The greedy giant ate the **whole** cake.*
3) *The **total** bill came to £50.*
4) *The **entire** audience started to clap.*

contain verb

To **contain** is to have something inside.
*This carton **contains** a litre of milk.*

> 1) **hold** 2) **consist** 3) **include** 4) **comprise**

1) *This bag **holds** 30 coloured marbles.*
2) *A stew usually **consists** of meat and vegetables.*
3) *The prize **includes** a car and a trip to Florida.*
4) *Our holiday **comprises** a week in Spain and a week in France.*

cook verb

When you **cook**, you prepare food by heating it.
Every evening my dad likes to cook dinner.

> 1) **make** 2) **heat** 3) **prepare**

1) *Grandma can make lots of different kinds of soup.*
2) *Mum heats the pizzas in the oven.*
3) *The chef prepared a banquet for 500 people.*

correct adjective

If something is **correct**, it is right.
The cashier gave me the correct change.

> 1) **right** 2) **accurate** 3) **true** 4) **precise**

1) *I gave the right answer to the teacher's question.*
2) *The boy gave an accurate description of the accident.*
3) *The man took off the mask to reveal his true identity.*
4) *This gold watch always tells the precise time.*

Opposites: **incorrect, wrong**

cosy adjective

Cosy means warm and snug.
We were cosy sitting in front of the fire.

> 1) **comfortable** 2) **snug** 3) **warm**

1) *The Davis family lives in a comfortable home.*
2) *The baby birds were snug inside their nest.*
3) *My thick, warm sweater keeps out the cold.*

count verb

When you **count**, you use numbers to find out how many things there are.
*My brother uses his fingers and thumbs to **count** to 10.*

> 1) **add** 2) **total** 3) **calculate**

1) *The waiter **added** up our bill.*
2) *The mechanic **totals** the cost of repairing the car.*
3) *The lorry driver **calculated** how much fuel he had left.*

crawl verb

To **crawl** is to move slowly along the ground on hands and knees.
*Babies **crawl** before they can walk.*

> 1) **creep** 2) **inch** 3) **slither** 4) **wriggle**

1) *The soldiers had to **creep** behind the enemy camp.*
2) *The climber began to **inch** his way along the narrow ledge.*
3) *Snakes **slither** along the ground.*
4) *Worms **wriggle** through the soil.*

creature noun

A **creature** is any animal.
*The blue whale is the world's biggest **creature**.*

> 1) **animal** 2) **beast** 3) **being**

1) *There are lots of **animals** in the city zoo.*
2) *We spotted the tracks of a wild **beast** in the forest.*
3) *Stories from ancient Greece are full of strange **beings**.*

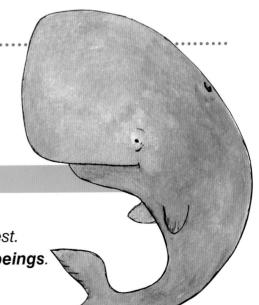

crisp adjective

If something is **crisp**, it is hard and dry.
*The biscuits were very **crisp** because we had baked them for too long.*

> 1) **hard** 2) **crunchy** 3) **firm**

1) *The **hard** toffee was difficult to chew.*
2) *Everyone likes eating **crunchy** popcorn.*
3) *The ground at the racetrack was **firm**.*

Opposite: **soft**

cross adjective

If you are **cross**, you are angry about something.
*The passengers were **cross** because the train was late.*

> 1) **annoyed** 2) **angry** 3) **irritated** 4) **grumpy**

1) *The teacher was **annoyed** that the rain had ruined sports day.*
2) *The old man was **angry** with the noisy children.*
3) *The fisherman was **irritated** because he didn't catch any fish.*
4) *Jacob was a **grumpy** boy who never seemed to smile.*

cruel adjective

If you are **cruel**, you are unkind to other people or to animals.
*The **cruel** boys kicked the old dog.*

> 1) **brutal** 2) **heartless** 3) **vicious** 4) **ruthless**

1) *The **brutal** man was always in fights.*
2) *The **heartless** thief stole the family's photographs.*
3) *The **vicious** dog attacked the kittens.*
4) *The **ruthless** gangster didn't care who got hurt in the fight.*

Opposites: **gentle, kind**

crush verb

To **crush** something is to squash it by pressing hard.
*You should **crush** the cans before you put them in the recycling bin.*

> 1) **flatten** 2) **squash** 3) **compress** 4) **mash**

1) *The dog **flattened** the flowers with his huge paws.*
2) *Luke had to **squash** his clothes into a small suitcase.*
3) *A huge machine **compresses** the old cars into scrap metal.*
4) *You can **mash** boiled potatoes with milk and butter.*

cry verb

When you **cry**, tears fall from your eyes.
*When Katy hurt her knee she began to **cry**.*

> 1) **weep** 2) **sob** 3) **howl** 4) **whimper**

1) *A bride often **weeps** with happiness on her wedding day.*
2) *Millie **sobbed** because she had torn her new dress.*
3) *The children **howled** when their pet rabbit died.*
4) *Our dog **whimpers** when she hears thunder.*

Opposite: **laugh**

cut verb

To **cut** something is to divide it or open it with scissors or a knife.
*The mayor **cut** the ribbon around the new swimming pool.*

> 1) **carve** 2) **chop** 3) **clip** 4) **slice** 5) **trim**

1) *Many sculptors **carve** statues out of stone.*
2) *The woodcutter must **chop** a lot of wood.*
3) *Dad likes to **clip** the hedge to make it neat.*
4) *The chef **sliced** the vegetables with a huge knife.*
5) *I need to **trim** my hair because it's too long.*

Dd damage

damage verb

To **damage** something is to harm or spoil it.
*The storm **damaged** the old oak tree.*

> 1) **destroy** 2) **devastate** 3) **ruin** 4) **wreck**

1) *The flood **destroyed** the old bridge.*
2) *The strong winds will **devastate** the wheat crop.*
3) *Sam **ruined** his bicycle when he crashed into a wall.*
4) *The huge waves **wrecked** the tiny rowing boat.*

Opposites: **fix, mend, repair**

damp adjective

If something is **damp**, it is slightly wet.
*I'll hang the **damp** clothes on the line.*

> 1) **wet** 2) **moist** 3) **humid**

1) *The **wet** grass sparkled in the early morning sunlight.*
2) *The walls of the old cellar were **moist**.*
3) *After the rains, the air in the jungle seemed **humid**.*

Opposite: **dry**

danger noun

A **danger** is something that is not safe.
*Fred's old car was a **danger** on the road.*

> 1) **risk** 2) **threat** 3) **peril** 4) **hazard**

1) *The man took a **risk** when he dived into the icy lake.*
2) *The weather forecast says there is a **threat** of rain tomorrow.*
3) *The sailors were in **peril** because of the stormy seas.*
4) *In the winter, ice can be a **hazard** on the roads.*

dark adjective

Dark means there is no light.
*The street was **dark** until the lights were switched on.*

> 1) **dim** 2) **gloomy** 3) **murky** 4) **shadowy**

1) *It was **dim** inside the cinema.*
2) *The prison cell was **gloomy** and cold.*
3) *It was a **murky** morning because of the thick fog.*
4) *John thought he saw a **shadowy** figure by the wall.*

Opposites: **bright, light**

dead adjective

Dead means no longer alive.
*The **dead** deer lay in the middle of the forest.*

> 1) **deceased** 2) **lifeless** 3) **killed** 4) **departed**

1) *The **deceased** father left all his money to his children.*
2) *The girl carried her dog's **lifeless** body into the house.*
3) *Every year we remember the soldiers who were **killed** in World War II.*
4) *The old man missed his **departed** wife very badly.*

Opposite: **alive**

decide verb

When you **decide**, you choose what to do or have.
*She **decided** to buy the red roses.*

> 1) **choose** 2) **determine** 3) **resolve** 4) **conclude**

1) *I always **choose** vanilla ice cream for dessert.*
2) *Jack was **determined** to get to school early.*
3) *Mum **resolved** to stop eating snacks during the day.*
4) *The doctor **concluded** that her patient should go to hospital.*

Dd delicious

delicious adjective

Something that is **delicious** tastes very good.
*We ate a **delicious** meal in the Italian restaurant.*

> 1) **appetizing** 2) **tasty** 3) **scrumptious** 4) **yummy**

1) *They found Chinese food quite **appetizing**.*
2) *The meat from the barbecue was very **tasty**.*
3) *"Your homemade pizza tastes **scrumptious**!" said Naomi.*
4) *The children thought that Ben's birthday cake was **yummy**.*

Opposites: **horrible, unpleasant**

destroy verb

To **destroy** means to spoil or to ruin.
*Mr Jacobs had to **destroy** the letter after reading it.*

> 1) **demolish** 2) **knock down** 3) **ruin** 4) **wreck**

1) *The bulldozer will **demolish** the factory building.*
2) *The workers had to **knock down** the old house.*
3) *"You will **ruin** your new shoes in the rain," warned Dad.*
4) *The vandals **wrecked** the flower beds in the park.*

Opposites: **build, create**

different adjective

Something that is **different** is not the same.
*The twins like to wear **different** clothes.*

> 1) **opposite** 2) **contrasting** 3) **assorted** 4) **changed**

1) *Meg and her mum have **opposite** views about music.*
2) *Black and white are **contrasting** colours.*
3) *We ate **assorted** snacks at the party.*
4) *Dad was worried about my **changed** attitude to work.*

dig verb

To **dig** is to break up the soil with a spade or a shovel.
*Grandpa had to **dig** the vegetable patch.*

> 1) **burrow** 2) **excavate** 3) **scoop** 4) **tunnel**

1) *Moles like to **burrow** under the ground.*
2) *The students had to **excavate** the old Roman temple.*
3) *You **scoop** soil out of the ground when you plant bulbs.*
4) *The prisoners managed to **tunnel** underground and escape.*

dinosaur noun

A **dinosaur** is a creature that lived a long time ago and no longer exists.
*Long, long ago, **dinosaurs** roamed over the planet.*

brontosaurus

ichthyosaurus

triceratops

stegosaurus

tyrannosaurus

dirty adjective

Something that is **dirty** is not clean.
*Kate's shoes were very **dirty** after the walk.*

> 1) **filthy** 2) **grimy** 3) **grubby** 4) **muddy**

1) *The rags were **filthy** after I used them to clean the car.*
2) *These **grimy** windows have not been washed for years.*
3) *The children were **grubby** after playing in the yard.*
4) *It was fun jumping in the **muddy** puddle.*

Opposite: **clean**

disaster noun

A **disaster** is an event that causes great loss or suffering.
*The famine caused a **disaster** in such a poor country.*

> 1) **accident** 2) **catastrophe** 3) **calamity**

1) *Tom broke his leg in a skating **accident**.*
2) *The damage from the flood was a **catastrophe** for the islanders.*
3) *It was a **calamity** when I lost my passport on holiday.*

discover verb

To **discover** is to find something or to find out about it.
*Patrick **discovered** some old coins in the garden.*

> 1) **find** 2) **detect** 3) **unearth** 4) **uncover**

1) *It took ages for Daniel to **find** his trainers.*
2) *Sherlock Holmes **detected** lots of crimes.*
3) *The dog **unearthed** the bone he had buried.*
4) *The historian hoped to **uncover** some prehistoric remains.*

dislike verb

If you **dislike** something or someone, you do not like that thing or person.
*My mum really **dislikes** spiders.*

1) **detest** 2) **hate** 3) **loathe**

1) *I **detest** rainy days.*
2) *The children **hate** it when their swimming lesson is cancelled.*
3) *The teacher says she **loathes** children with bad manners.*

Opposite: **like**

dive verb

To **dive** is to move quickly downwards, often head first.
*The penguins **dive** into the water one at a time.*

1) **drop** 2) **plunge** 3) **swoop**

1) *The damaged plane began to **drop** towards the ground.*
2) *Jim and Jack **plunged** into the pool.*
3) *The birds **swoop** down to get food from the bird table.*

do verb

If you **do** something, you go ahead with it and finish it.
*My brother likes to **do** his exercises every morning.*

1) **carry out** 2) **perform** 3) **achieve** 4) **complete**

1) *The servants had to **carry out** lots of duties in the emperor's palace.*
2) *Our dog can **perform** funny tricks.*
3) *Max **achieved** four lengths of the swimming pool in record time.*
4) *I **completed** the marathon in just under four hours.*

doubt verb

If you **doubt**, you are not sure about something or someone.
*Kelly began to **doubt** that she would get to school on time.*

> 1) **suspect** 2) **mistrust** 3) **hesitate** 4) **question**

1) *The judge **suspected** the witness's account.*
2) *The nurse **mistrusted** our reasons for wanting to help.*
3) *The driver **hesitated** about which road to take.*
4) *The scientists tried to **question** the researcher's findings.*

Opposites: **believe, trust**

draw verb

When you **draw** you use a pencil or crayon to make a picture.
*This artist likes to **draw** tropical birds.*

> 1) **sketch** 2) **trace** 3) **doodle**

1) *The art class tried to **sketch** the flowers on the table.*
2) *Ben **traced** the design onto his book.*
3) *My little sister has **doodled** all over my English textbook.*

draw verb

If something **draws** you, you want to move closer to it.
*The film star always **draws** a huge crowd of fans.*

> 1) **attract** 2) **bring** 3) **entice** 4) **pull in**

1) *Colourful plants in the garden **attract** butterflies.*
2) *The reduced prices **brought** lots of customers to the shop.*
3) *Mum **enticed** the kitten down from the tree with a bowl of milk.*
4) *The opening night of the show **pulled in** a huge audience.*

dry adjective

If something is **dry**, it is not wet.
*Ben put on **dry** clothes after his swimming lesson.*

> 1) **arid** 2) **parched** 3) **thirsty**

1) *Only a few trees grew on the **arid** land.*
2) *The fields were **parched** because it had not rained for months.*
3) *Ted was **thirsty** after playing tennis in the hot sunshine.*

Opposite: **wet**

dull adjective

Dull means not interesting.
*Catherine was reading a really **dull** book.*

> 1) **boring** 2) **dreary** 3) **tedious** 4) **uninteresting**

1) *The children thought the science lesson was **boring**.*
2) *The visit to the museum was **dreary**.*
3) *The play was very long and **tedious**.*
4) *Dad says the newspaper is full of **uninteresting** stories.*

Opposites: **exciting, interesting**

dull adjective

Dull means not bright or clear.
*It was a **dull** day because the sun wasn't shining.*

> 1) **cloudy** 2) **gloomy** 3) **drab** 4) **dismal**

1) *After a **cloudy** morning, bright sunshine appeared in the afternoon.*
2) *The **gloomy** room had only one tiny window.*
3) *The old lady wore **drab** clothes.*
4) *Everyone stayed inside because of the **dismal** weather.*

eager adjective

If you are **eager**, you really want to do or have something.
*The football team was **eager** to start the game.*

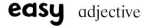

> 1) **enthusiastic** 2) **impatient** 3) **keen**

1) *The audience was very **enthusiastic** about the new band.*
2) *The passengers were **impatient** to board the plane.*
3) *Clare was **keen** to practise her ice skating.*

easy adjective

Easy means not difficult.
*We thought the maths test was **easy**.*

> 1) **clear** 2) **simple** 3) **straightforward** 4) **plain**

1) *The leaflet gave **clear** instructions for building the model plane.*
2) *The chemistry experiment was **simple** once the teacher had explained it.*
3) *The directions to our new house are very **straightforward**.*
4) *The computer manual was written in **plain** language.*

Opposites: **difficult, hard**

eat verb

When you **eat** you chew food and then swallow it.
*My grandma likes to **eat** eggs for breakfast.*

> 1) **chew** 2) **consume** 3) **munch** 4) **swallow**

1) *Mum told Fred to **chew** his food properly.*
2) *Our dogs **consume** a lot of food each day.*
3) *Horses like to **munch** hay.*
4) *After you have chewed your food you **swallow** it.*

empty adjective

If something is **empty**, it has nothing or no one in it.
*The box was **empty** because we had eaten all the chocolates.*

> 1) **bare** 2) **vacant** 3) **unoccupied** 4) **hollow**

1) *The floor was **bare** with no carpet or rugs on it.*
2) *The house was **vacant** after the students moved out.*
3) *The old mansion has been **unoccupied** for many years.*
4) *A family of owls lives inside the **hollow** tree trunk.*

Opposite: **full**

end noun

The **end** of something is the last part of it.
*The audience clapped at the **end** of the concert.*

> 1) **ending** 2) **finish** 3) **conclusion**

1) *The crime novel had a really exciting **ending**.*
2) *There was an exciting **finish** to this year's marathon.*
3) *The meeting came to a quick **conclusion** when the protesters walked in.*

Opposites: **beginning, start**

end verb

If something **ends**, it stops or finishes.
*Our school term **ends** at the beginning of July.*

> 1) **finish** 2) **conclude** 3) **stop** 4) **cease**

1) *Matthew **finished** his homework before going out to play.*
2) *The concert **concluded** with a piano solo.*
3) *The rain finally **stopped** after lunch.*
4) *The fighting **ceased** when the police arrived.*

Opposites: **begin, start**

enjoy verb

If you **enjoy** something, you really like doing it.
*Tim and Kelly **enjoy** watching television.*

> 1) **appreciate** 2) **like** 3) **love**

1) *My parents **appreciate** the good food in the Japanese restaurant.*
2) *We **like** to eat outdoors in the summer.*
3) *The twins **love** visiting the local farm.*

Opposites: **detest, hate, loathe**

enormous adjective

Enormous means very big.
*Tyrannosaurus rex was an **enormous** dinosaur.*

> 1) **gigantic** 2) **huge** 3) **giant** 4) **massive**

1) *A **gigantic** wave swept over the ship.*
2) *A **huge** rock fell from the cliff.*
3) *The explorers found some **giant** footprints in the snow.*
4) *Mount Everest is a **massive** mountain.*

Opposites: **little, small, tiny**

enough adjective

If you have **enough** of something, you have as much as you need.
*Mum bought **enough** food to last the whole week.*

> 1) **ample** 2) **adequate** 3) **sufficient**

1) *The greengrocer had an **ample** supply of apples.*
2) *There was **adequate** food for all the children at the school picnic.*
3) *There is a **sufficient** supply of water on the island.*

Opposites: **inadequate, insufficient**

enter verb

To **enter** is to go in or to come in.
*The knights could **enter** the castle through
a secret passageway.*

> 1) **come in** 2) **go in** 3) **arrive**

1) *Dad **came in** through the front door.*
2) *The nurse called our names to **go in** to
see the doctor.*
3) *The actress **arrived** by the stage door.*

even adjective

If something is **even**, it is flat and smooth.
*The new linoleum was more **even** than the old carpet.*

> 1) **flat** 2) **smooth** 3) **level**

1) *The paper was folded into a **flat** shape.*
2) *The girl had **smooth**, shiny hair.*
3) *A **level** pathway led to the metal gate.*

Opposites: **bumpy, rough**

even adjective

If two things are **even**, it means they are the same.
*Jack and Luke had **even** scores in the maths test.*

> 1) **the same** 2) **level** 3) **equal**

1) *Mary and Beth wore **the same** dresses.*
2) *The painting on the wall was **level** with the bookcase.*
3) *The twins were given **equal** amounts of money for their birthday.*

Opposite: **different**

evil adjective

Evil means bad or wicked.
*The **evil** witch stood by her cauldron to cast a spell.*

1) **bad** 2) **wicked** 3) **hateful** 4) **wrong**

1) *The **bad** soldiers were punished by the general.*
2) *The burglar was **wicked** to steal from the old lady.*
3) *The cruel man was **hateful** to his old dog.*
4) *It is **wrong** to steal from other people.*

Opposite: **good**

excellent adjective

Excellent means very good.
*Jack got **excellent** grades in his report.*

1) **outstanding** 2) **superb** 3) **wonderful**

1) *Emma trained hard to become an
   outstanding rider.*
2) *Lucy played a **superb** game of tennis.*
3) *Everyone had a **wonderful** time at
   my birthday party.*

excited adjective

Excited means happy and lively.
*Our puppy gets very **excited** when we play with her.*

1) **lively** 2) **thrilled** 3) **boisterous**

1) *The playground was full of **lively** children.*
2) *The boy was **thrilled** by the magician's amazing tricks.*
3) *Sam and Michael were so **boisterous** that they broke a chair.*

Opposites: **bored, dull**

explain *verb*

To **explain** is to make something easy to understand.
*The instructor tried to **explain** how to use the new running machine.*

> 1) **clarify** 2) **make clear** 3) **demonstrate**

1) *The manager **clarified** what to do when the fire alarm rings.*
2) *Mr Jones **made clear** that he expected us to behave well on the trip.*
3) *The chef **demonstrated** how to make perfect pastry.*

extinct *adjective*

If an animal is **extinct**, there are no more of that kind alive on Earth.
*Dinosaurs became **extinct** millions of years ago.*

> 1) **lost** 2) **vanished**

1) *No one had seen the **lost** tribe for many years.*
2) *Two kinds of Asian tiger are now **vanished** species.*

Opposite: **living**

extraordinary *adjective*

Something that is **extraordinary** is very unusual.
*Fred's aunt is wearing an **extraordinary** hat.*

> 1) **amazing** 2) **bizarre** 3) **strange** 4) **unusual**

1) *Jim did an **amazing** dive into the pool.*
2) *Todd got a **bizarre** present from his grandfather.*
3) *Our local novelty store sells **strange** things.*
4) *The **unusual** design for the new school building won first prize.*

Opposites: **ordinary, usual**

faint adjective

Someone or something that is **faint** is not strong.
*The pictures in the old book were very **faint**.*

> 1) **weak** 2) **pale** 3) **dim**

1) *The summer heat made Grandma feel **weak**.*
2) *The nursery walls were painted in very **pale** colours.*
3) *The travellers could see a **dim** light in the distance.*

Opposites: **bold, distinct, strong**

fair adjective

If something is **fair**, it seems to be reasonable and the right thing to do.
*A football referee has to be **fair** to both teams.*

> 1) **just** 2) **equal** 3) **right** 4) **proper**

1) *The prisoner received a **just** punishment for his crime.*
2) *Mum gave us **equal** amounts of ice cream.*
3) *Everyone agreed that Jack was the **right** choice for team captain.*
4) *The jury tried to make **proper** decisions about the court case.*

Opposite: **unfair**

fall verb

To **fall** is to move downwards quickly.
*The parachutist started to **fall** back down to the ground.*

> 1) **drop** 2) **descend** 3) **dive** 4) **plunge**

1) *When it's windy the leaves **drop** off the trees.*
2) *The lift **descends** to the next floor in the store.*
3) *The children wanted to **dive** into the deep end of the pool.*
4) *Kingfishers **plunge** to grab fish from the water.*

Opposite: **rise**

famous adjective

Someone who is **famous** is well known to lots of people.
*The **famous** pop star performed for her fans.*

1) **well known** 2) **eminent** 3) **celebrated**

1) *Have you ever spotted a **well-known** film star in the street?*
2) *The **eminent** scientist won a Nobel prize.*
3) *The **celebrated** artist held an
   exhibition of his work.*

fantastic adjective

Fantastic means absolutely wonderful.
*Beth's new party shoes are **fantastic**.*

1) **amazing** 2) **far-fetched** 3) **extraordinary** 3) **incredible**

1) *I'm reading an **amazing** book about dragons and unicorns.*
2) *The science-fiction author wrote some **far-fetched** stories.*
3) *The actresses wore some **extraordinary** costumes.*
4) *My uncle told us about his **incredible** adventures.*

faraway adjective

Something that is **faraway** is not near.
*Pluto is a **faraway** planet.*

1) **distant** 2) **remote** 3) **outlying**

1) *Dan could see the **distant** hills on the horizon.*
2) *The shepherd lived in a **remote** cottage on the mountain.*
3) *The floods cut off an **outlying** farm for three days.*

Opposite: **near**

fast adjective

Someone or something that is **fast** can move quickly.
*The **fast** cars sped around the racetrack.*

> 1) **quick** 2) **speedy** 3) **rapid** 4) **swift**

1) *I take the dog for a **quick** walk every morning.*
2) *Dad's new car was very **speedy** in traffic.*
3) *The **rapid** train reaches London in less than two hours.*
4) *The gazelle is a **swift** and graceful animal.*

Opposite: **slow**

fat adjective

Fat means big and rounded.
*Bert is **fat** because he eats too many chips!*

> 1) **plump** 2) **chubby** 3) **overweight** 4) **tubby**

1) *Dad roasted a **plump** chicken for dinner.*
2) *Carl had a **chubby** pig as a pet.*
3) *George is so **overweight** that he can't fit into his clothes.*
4) *Ellie's teddy bear is very **tubby**.*

Opposites: **slim, thin**

fear noun

You feel **fear** when you think something bad is about to happen to you.
*We shook with **fear** when we thought we saw a ghost.*

> 1) **fright** 2) **terror** 3) **dread** 4) **alarm**

1) *Ben gave his sister a **fright** when he jumped out of the cupboard.*
2) *The scary film filled the audience with **terror**.*
3) *My mum has a real **dread** of spiders.*
4) *The guard raised the **alarm** when the fire started.*

feel verb

If you **feel** something, you touch it to see what it's like.
*Thick, woolly blankets **feel** soft and warm.*

> 1) **touch** 2) **finger** 3) **pet**

1) *You must not **touch** the displays in the museum.*
2) *I like to **finger** the little stones on Mum's bracelet.*
3) *Kittens purr when you **pet** them.*

fierce adjective

Fierce means angry and dangerous.
*The **fierce** dog barked at the postman.*

> 1) **dangerous** 2) **ferocious** 3) **savage** 4) **vicious**

1) *The hippopotamus is a large and **dangerous** animal.*
2) *The mother tiger behaved in a **ferocious** way.*
3) *A **savage** lion was stalking the herd of zebras.*
4) *The guard dog is **vicious** if you get too close to it.*

Opposite: **gentle**

fight verb

If you **fight** someone, you try to hurt that person.
*The two armies were about to **fight** over the disputed land.*

> 1) **battle** 2) **struggle** 3) **brawl** 4) **grapple**

1) *In olden days knights used to **battle** on horseback.*
2) *The two girls **struggled** over the new CD player.*
3) *The rival gangs were **brawling** in the streets.*
4) *The two warriors **grappled** with each other.*

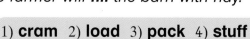

fill verb

If you **fill** something, you make it full.
*The farmer will **fill** the barn with hay.*

> 1) **cram** 2) **load** 3) **pack** 4) **stuff**

1) *It is rude to **cram** your mouth with food.*
2) *The men **loaded** the furniture into the moving van.*
3) *The dentist **packed** lots of appointments into her busy day.*
4) *Mum will **stuff** the toy horse with a special filling.*

Opposites: **clear out, empty**

find verb

When you **find** someone or something, you come across what you have been looking for.
*Josh had to search everywhere to **find** his football boots.*

> 1) **notice** 2) **spot** 3) **trace** 4) **discover**

1) *I **noticed** the lost kitten under a bush.*
2) *A stolen car was **spotted** at the end of the street.*
3) *My aunt has been trying to **trace** her long-lost brother for years.*
4) *The walkers had to **discover** the way home for themselves.*

Opposite: **lose**

finish verb

When you **finish** something, you come to the end of it.
*Peter was the last person to **finish** the sack race.*

> 1) **end** 2) **conclude** 3) **stop**

1) *The film **ended** at 10 o'clock.*
2) *The show **concluded** with a big chorus.*
3) *Grandma told us to **stop** being so noisy.*

Opposites: **begin, start**

fix verb

If you **fix** something, you make it work again.
*Katy had to **fix** her punctured tyre.*

> 1) **repair** 2) **mend** 3) **patch**

1) *The garage will **repair** my damaged car.*
2) *Dad **mended** the broken desk lamp.*
3) *Grandpa **patched** the broken window
   in his greenhouse.*

Opposite: **break**

fly verb

To **fly** is to move through the air.
*Most birds use their wings to **fly**.*

> 1) **soar** 2) **glide** 3) **swoop** 4) **float**

1) *Eagles **soar** high into the sky.*
2) *The plane started to **glide** towards the runway.*
3) *The gull **swooped** down and caught a fish.*
4) *A feather will **float** slowly down to the ground.*

fog noun

Fog is a thick, misty air that you cannot see through.
*He switched on the car headlights in the thick **fog**.*

> 1) **mist** 2) **haze** 3) **smog**

1) *An early morning **mist** hung over the sea.*
2) *The trees seemed to shimmer in the **haze**.*
3) *The driver found it hard to find his way in the thick **smog**.*

follow verb

If you **follow**, you move along behind a person or thing.
*The children **follow** their teacher into the classroom.*

> 1) **pursue** 2) **chase** 3) **trail** 4) **track**

1) *The police officer **pursued** the burglar.*
2) *Our dog likes to **chase** cats.*
3) *The private detective **trailed** the main suspect.*
4) *The ranger **tracked** the animals across the plain.*

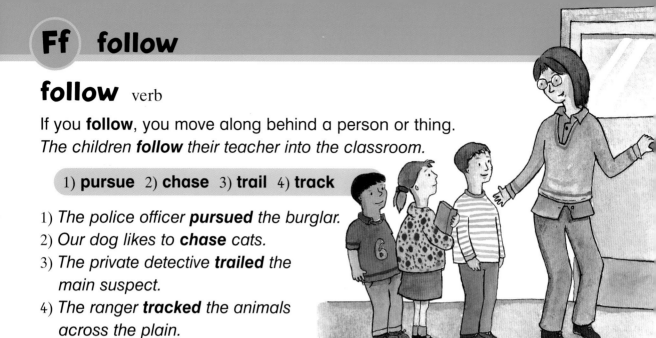

food noun

Food is what you eat to stay alive and well.
*Mum bought lots of **food** at the supermarket.*

fruit

bread

vegetables

meat

fish

cakes

eggs

salad

ice cream

forget verb

If you **forget** something, you do not remember it.
*Do not **forget** to feed your pet every day.*

> 1) **ignore** 2) **omit** 3) **overlook**

1) *Sarah tried to **ignore** the bully in her class.*
2) *The airline **omitted** some names from the passenger list.*
3) *The teacher said he would **overlook** Joe's bad behaviour this time.*

Opposite: **remember**

free adjective

If something is **free**, you do not have to pay money for it.
*The tickets to the open-air concert were **free**.*

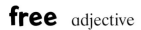

> 1) **complimentary** 2) **on the house**

1) *We were given **complimentary** tickets to the theatre.*
2) *The new restaurant owner gave his first customers a meal **on the house**.*

free adjective

If something is **free**, it is not being used.
*The seat next to me was **free**.*

> 1) **available** 2) **vacant** 3) **unoccupied**

1) *The next **available** flight from Bristol was at 2 pm.*
2) *I asked the hotel manager if he had any **vacant** rooms for the night.*
3) *We couldn't find any **unoccupied** seats on the train.*

Opposites: **in use, occupied, taken**

friend noun

A **friend** is someone you know and like.
*Sarah is Rosie's best **friend**.*

> 1) **pal** 2) **companion** 3) **ally**

1) *Tom missed his **pals** when he moved house.*
2) *Mrs Brown's dog was a good **companion**.*
3) *France and America were Britain's **allies** in World War II.*

Opposite: **enemy**

frighten verb

If you **frighten** someone, you scare that person.
*My friend Josh tried to **frighten** me with a toy spider.*

> 1) **alarm** 2) **scare** 3) **startle** 4) **terrify**

1) *If you jump out at people you **alarm** them.*
2) *The spooky film **scared** the audience.*
3) *If you **startle** a horse it may rear up.*
4) *Big snakes **terrify** many people.*

Opposites: **calm, reassure**

frown verb

If you **frown**, you make an angry face at someone or something.
*The professor **frowned** when the students talked during his lecture.*

> 1) **glare** 2) **scowl** 3) **glower** 4) **grimace**

1) *Mum **glared** at me because my room was so messy.*
2) *The goalkeeper **scowled** when the other team scored.*
3) *The general **glowered** at the soldiers in front of him.*
4) *The runners **grimaced** as they crossed the finish line.*

fruit noun

A **fruit** is the part of a plant that you can eat.
*Most **fruits** are sweet and juicy.*

apples
oranges
bananas
strawberries
grapes
pineapple
pears
peaches

full adjective

If something is **full**, it contains as much as possible.
*The suitcase was **full** of holiday clothes.*

1) **filled** 2) **crammed** 3) **crowded** 4) **packed**

1) *The bag was **filled** with groceries.*
2) *The library is **crammed** with new books.*
3) *The streets of London are very **crowded**.*
4) *The stadium was **packed** with fans.*

Opposites: **empty, incomplete**

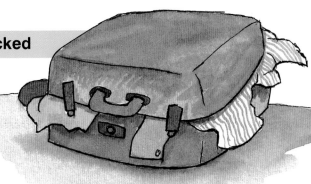

funny adjective

Something that is **funny** makes you laugh.
*Simon told his friends a **funny** joke.*

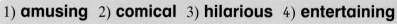

> 1) **amusing** 2) **comical** 3) **hilarious** 4) **entertaining**

1) *There are some **amusing** cartoons in this magazine.*
2) *The clown made everyone laugh with his **comical** dance.*
3) *Everyone enjoyed the **hilarious** movie.*
4) *The Lion King is a very **entertaining** show.*

Opposites: **sad, serious**

funny adjective

Something that is **funny** is a little surprising or out of the ordinary.
*Sam had a **funny** feeling that someone was following him.*

> 1) **odd** 2) **peculiar** 3) **strange** 4) **unusual**

1) *The art teacher liked to wear **odd** clothes.*
2) *We found a **peculiar** shell on the beach.*
3) *Jasmine saw a **strange** car in the street.*
4) *Mum wore an **unusual** hat to my sister's wedding.*

fuss noun

A **fuss** is a disturbance.
*There was a big **fuss** when the cow fell into the pond.*

> 1) **commotion** 2) **uproar** 3) **trouble**

1) *The fire in the main street caused a big **commotion**.*
2) *There was an **uproar** when the concert was cancelled.*
3) *Dad made **trouble** when the barber cut his hair
   too short.*

generous adjective

A **generous** person enjoys giving to others.
The generous boss gave everyone fabulous Christmas presents.

> 1) **magnanimous** 2) **liberal** 3) **charitable** 4) **lavish**

1) *The **magnanimous** executive gave lots of money to charity.*
2) *The teacher was very **liberal** with his time.*
3) *The oil company gave **charitable** gifts to good causes.*
4) *Amy's mother was **lavish** with her praise.*

gentle adjective

Someone who is **gentle** is soft and kind.
The gentle girl picked up the kitten.

> 1) **soft** 2) **mild** 3) **tender**

1) *The announcer spoke in a **soft** voice.*
2) *There was a **mild** breeze at the coast.*
3) *Hannah gave her puppy a **tender** pat.*

Opposites: **harsh, rough**

get verb

If you **get** something, you receive it or have it.
Jess hopes to get a new bike for her birthday.

> 1) **acquire** 2) **obtain** 3) **earn** 4) **receive**

1) *Alison **acquired** her grandmother's jewels.*
2) *Everyone wants to **obtain** the latest computer games.*
3) *I am going to **earn** a lot of money by babysitting.*
4) *Jenny **received** a new book from her aunt.*

Opposite: **lose**

gift noun

A **gift** is a present that someone gives to you.
*Robert could not wait to open his **gift**.*

> 1) **present** 2) **donation** 3) **bonus**

1) *Her birthday **present** was a new dress.*
2) *The electronics company gave a big **donation** to the famine appeal.*
3) *The employees got a **bonus** from their boss.*

give verb

To **give** means to let someone have something.
*Dad likes to **give** Mum flowers on her birthday.*

> 1) **grant** 2) **present** 3) **donate** 4) **provide**

1) *The good fairy **granted** three wishes to the princess.*
2) *The referee **presented** the prize to the winning team.*
3) *We were asked to **donate** money to the charity.*
4) *The teacher **provided** us with the answers.*

Opposites: **receive, take**

glad adjective

If you are **glad**, you are pleased and happy.
*I'm **glad** that my favourite cousin is coming to stay.*

> 1) **pleased** 2) **delighted** 3) **happy** 4) **joyful**

1) *Dan was **pleased** with his new skateboard.*
2) *Grandma was **delighted** to see all her grandchildren.*
3) *The children had a **happy** vacation at the beach.*
4) *Ellie wished all her friends a very **joyful** Christmas.*

Opposites: **sad, unhappy**

glow   noun

A **glow** is a warm shine.
*The hotel dining room had a warm, welcoming **glow**.*

> 1) **glimmer** 2) **radiance** 3) **shine**

1) *There was a **glimmer** in the singer's eyes.*
2) *Everyone noticed the bride's **radiance** on her wedding day.*
3) *James polished his shoes to give them a **shine**.*

go   verb

To **go** is to move toward or away from something.
*Mum said it was time to **go** to bed.*

> 1) **depart** 2) **leave** 3) **set off**

1) *The train will **depart** from platform six.*
2) *We had to **leave** the house at three o'clock.*
3) *My parents **set off** for the beach.*

Opposites: **remain, stay**

go   noun

To give something a **go** means to try it.
*Last year I gave skateboarding a **go**.*

> 1) **try** 2) **effort** 3) **attempt**

1) *Dad persuaded me to give football a **try**.*
2) *We made an **effort** to play our new board game.*
3) *The archer hit the bullseye on the first **attempt**.*

Gg good

good adjective

If you are **good** you behave well.
*She was a **good** girl at the party.*

> 1) **well behaved** 2) **polite** 3) **virtuous** 4) **obedient**

1) *The class was **well behaved** on the school trip.*
2) *Peter was a **polite** boy.*
3) *King Frederick was a **virtuous** ruler.*
4) *Laura has a very **obedient** dog.*

Opposite: **naughty**

good adjective

If something is **good**, it is of the best quality.
*We watched a **good** film last night.*

> 1) **excellent** 2) **super** 3) **first class** 4) **splendid**

1) *The pianist was an **excellent** musician.*
2) *Mum cooked a **super** meal.*
3) *The TV show was **first class**.*
4) *Michael made a **splendid** model of a monster.*

Opposite: **bad**

grab verb

If you **grab** something, you take it quickly.
*The thief tried to **grab** my purse.*

> 1) **seize** 2) **take** 3) **snatch** 4) **pluck**

1) *The captain tried to **seize** the stowaways.*
2) *The pirates **took** the treasure and sailed away.*
3) *It is rude to **snatch** when someone hands you something.*
4) *The sailor leaned over the side to **pluck** the girl from the water.*

grand adjective

Something that is **grand** seems very important.
The King and Queen looked very grand.

> 1) **dignified** 2) **impressive** 3) **glorious** 4) **majestic**

1) *Ben's dad looked **dignified** in his new suit.*
2) *The visitors thought the palace was very **impressive**.*
3) *The old people had a **glorious** day out
   in the country.*
4) *The opera singer wore very **majestic** clothes.*

Opposites: **humble, modest**

great adjective

If something is **great**, it is large in size or in number.
There was a great steeple on top of the church.

> 1) **big** 2) **immense** 3) **enormous** 4) **vast**

1) *The **big** cruise ship sailed into the harbour.*
2) *The researcher had an **immense** knowledge of his subject.*
3) *The young vet had an **enormous** love of animals.*
4) *A **vast** crowd gathered to see the parade.*

Opposites: **little, small, tiny**

greedy adjective

If you are **greedy**, you eat more than your fair share.
The greedy boy ate the whole cake.

> 1) **gluttonous** 2) **voracious** 3) **selfish**

1) *The **gluttonous** pig never stopped eating.*
2) *The **voracious** queen wanted more food than anyone else.*
3) *The **selfish** boy would not share his sweets with his sister.*

group noun

A **group** is a collection of people, animals, or things.

*A small **group** of singers is called a choir.*

a gaggle of geese

a swarm of bees

a pride of lions

a school of fish

a flock of sheep

a parliament of owls

a herd of cows

a pack of hounds

grow verb

When something **grows** it gets bigger.
*The sunflowers started to **grow** above the wall.*

> 1) **develop** 2) **increase** 3) **swell**

1) *Small seeds **develop** into leafy plants.*
2) *The fund for the new school quickly **increased**.*
3) *The balloon **swelled** as I blew into it.*

Opposite: **shrink**

guess verb

If you **guess** something, you think it is right, but you are not sure.
*The burglar **guessed** where the key was hidden.*

> 1) **think** 2) **estimate** 3) **suspect**

1) *I **think** I might get a new surfboard for my birthday.*
2) *The carpenter **estimated** that it would take a week to make the cabinet.*
3) *The police officer **suspected** that the mystery thief was a man.*

guide verb

If you **guide** someone, you show that person how to do or find something.
*The local people **guided** the explorers through the jungle.*

> 1) **direct** 2) **lead** 3) **accompany** 4) **usher**

1) *The police officer **directed** the traffic.*
2) *The firefighter **led** the patients out of the burning hospital.*
3) *My older sister **accompanied** us to the sports centre.*
4) *The officials **ushered** the athletes into the sports village.*

handsome adjective

A **handsome** person is good looking.
*The **handsome** prince had married a beautiful princess.*

> 1) **attractive** 2) **fine** 3) **good looking**

1) *The bride and groom made an **attractive** couple.*
2) *The model had a very **fine** face.*
3) *Mrs Allen was proud of her **good-looking** son.*

Opposite: **ugly**

happen verb

If something **happens**, it occurs or takes place.
*Accidents can **happen** if you take risks.*

> 1) **take place** 2) **occur** 3) **come about** 4) **arise**

1) *Jamie's party **took place** at the bowling alley.*
2) *Your birthday **occurs** on the same date each year.*
3) *Flooding may **come about** after a heavy storm.*
4) *An argument **arose** between the two football teams.*

happy adjective

If you are **happy**, you feel pleased.
*Sarah had a very **happy** eighth birthday.*

> 1) **blissful** 2) **contented** 3) **delighted** 4) **thrilled**

1) *The children had a **blissful** holiday at the lake.*
2) *Mark was a very **contented** baby.*
3) *I was **delighted** to get an invitation to
   the opening of the new art gallery.*
4) *Josh was **thrilled** to get a part in the
   school play.*

Opposites: **sad, unhappy**

hard adjective

If something is **hard**, it is very difficult.
*The students did not like the **hard** maths test.*

> 1) **tough** 2) **difficult** 3) **demanding**

1) *It was **tough** work planting the new trees.*
2) *It was **difficult** to find a cure for the disease.*
3) *The teacher gave us some **demanding** homework.*

Opposite: **easy**

hard adjective

A **hard** object is firm and solid.
*The bridge was made of **hard** concrete.*

> 1) **rigid** 2) **firm** 3) **unyielding**

1) *The fragile statue was packed in a **rigid** container.*
2) *You have to put bathroom scales on a **firm** surface.*
3) *It was impossible to push open the **unyielding** door.*

Opposite: **soft**

harm verb

To **harm** means to hurt someone or something.
*Alex was careful not to **harm** the butterfly.*

> 1) **damage** 2) **hurt** 3) **injure** 4) **ruin**

1) *Very strong winds may **damage** buildings.*
2) *When the horse fell over it **hurt** its leg.*
3) *It is cruel to **injure** animals.*
4) *Spilling milk onto a table will **ruin** the wood.*

Opposites: **benefit, help**

hat noun

A **hat** is an item of clothing that you wear on your head.
*I tried on an interesting **hat** in the store.*

baseball cap

bobble hat

bonnet

deerstalker

panama

top hat

sun hat

hate adjective

If you **hate** something, you do not like it at all.
*We **hate** eating Brussels sprouts.*

1) **despise** 2) **detest** 3) **dislike** 4) **loathe**

1) *We all **despise** bullies at school.*
2) *Some people **detest** spiders.*
3) *I **dislike** doing my homework.*
4) *Kelly **loathes** tidying her bedroom.*

Opposites: **like, love**

have verb

If you **have** something, it belongs to you.
*I **have** a rabbit called Floppy.*

1) **own** 2) **possess** 3) **hold**

1) *Susie **owns** five teddy bears.*
2) *Dad **possessed** hundreds of books.*
3) *The winning team **holds** the sports trophy for a year.*

heal verb

To **heal** is to get better or to make something or
someone better.
*A doctor tries to **heal** his patients.*

1) **cure** 2) **soothe** 3) **mend**

1) *The ointment **cured** the itchy rash.*
2) *Mum **soothed** my sore throat with honey and lemon.*
3) *After four weeks her broken arm **mended**.*

Opposites: **harm, hurt**

heavy adjective

Something that is **heavy** is difficult to lift up.
*I helped carry the **heavy** shopping bags.*

1) **hefty** 2) **cumbersome** 3) **bulky** 4) **weighty**

1) *The old man could not lift the **hefty** box.*
2) *The movers tried to carry the **cumbersome** chest.*
3) *The set of encyclopedias is packed in a **bulky** carton.*
4) *A St Bernard is a **weighty** dog.*

Opposite: **light**

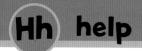

help verb

If you **help** someone, you assist that person.
*The police officer **helped** the blind woman cross the street.*

> 1) **aid** 2) **assist** 3) **support**

1) *Some people use a cane to **aid** walking.*
2) *We offered to **assist** the new teacher.*
3) *The social worker **supports** families who are in trouble.*

Opposite: **hinder**

hide verb

To **hide** means to keep out of sight.
*Mother leopards **hide** their cubs in bushes and under rocks.*

> 1) **secrete** 2) **conceal** 3) **cover up**

1) *The smugglers decided to **secrete** the barrels in a cave.*
2) *The fox **concealed** itself under the bush.*
3) *The accountant tried to **cover up** his mistakes.*

Opposites: **display, show**

high adjective

If something is **high**, it rises up above other things.
*It was the first time he had climbed a **high** mountain.*

> 1) **lofty** 2) **tall** 3) **towering**

1) *In New York there are many **lofty** skyscrapers.*
2) *Tina is **tall** for her age.*
3) *The new cathedral is a **towering** building.*

Opposites: **low, short**

hit verb

To **hit** something means to strike it.
*Ben can **hit** the ball a long way.*

> 1) **strike** 2) **punch** 3) **thump** 4) **batter**

1) *He did not want the bully to **strike** him.*
2) *The players like to **punch** the air when they score a goal.*
3) *Rabbits **thump** their hind legs on the ground when they sense danger.*
4) *The rain **battered** the window panes.*

hobby noun

A **hobby** is something you enjoy doing in your spare time.
*My new **hobby** is collecting old film posters.*

> 1) **pastime** 2) **interest** 3) **leisure activity**

1) *Tim's only **pastime** was playing golf.*
2) *She has a strong **interest** in bird watching.*
3) *Tennis is Lily's favourite **leisure activity**.*

hold verb

To **hold** something means to have it in your hands or arms.
*The farmer tried to **hold** the newborn lamb.*

> 1) **carry** 2) **cradle** 3) **grasp** 4) **clasp**

1) *The foreman asked us to **carry** the bricks.*
2) *The nurse **cradled** the newborn baby carefully.*
3) *Dad **grasped** the ladder while Mum climbed into the attic.*
4) *The toddler **clasped** his favourite teddy bear.*

Opposites: **let go, release**

home noun

Home is the place where you live.
*He loved his new **home** in the heart of the city.*

> 1) **dwelling** 2) **residence** 3) **abode**

1) *Their **dwelling** was small and cosy.*
2) *The doctor's summer **residence** is in Scotland.*
3) *The emigrants missed their old **abode**.*

horrible adjective

If something is **horrible**, it is very bad.
*Ella had a **horrible** cold.*

> 1) **dreadful** 2) **awful** 3) **unpleasant** 4) **nasty**

1) *The supervisor said their work was **dreadful**.*
2) *The butcher had an **awful** day at work.*
3) *The burnt food tasted really **unpleasant**.*
4) *She said some **nasty** things about her new neighbour.*

Opposites: **lovely, wonderful**

hot adjective

Hot is very warm.
*It's very **hot** on the beach in the summer.*

> 1) **scorching** 2) **burning** 3) **sweltering** 4) **scalding**

1) *The sun was **scorching** so I put on my hat.*
2) *The **burning** building fell to the ground.*
3) *Emma was **sweltering** in her woolly sweater.*
4) *The soup was **scalding**, so we waited for it to cool down.*

Opposite: **cold**

hungry adjective

When you are **hungry**, you need to eat food.
*The players were always **hungry** after sports practice.*

> 1) **ravenous** 2) **famished** 3) **starving**

1) *Dad was **ravenous**, so he bought a sandwich.*
2) *The walkers were **famished** after their long hike.*
3) *I didn't eat breakfast, so I was **starving** by lunchtime.*

hurry verb

To **hurry** means to move quickly.
*Dad had to **hurry** to catch the train.*

> 1) **rush** 2) **scurry** 3) **hasten** 4) **dash**

1) *We had to **rush** to school because we were late.*
2) *The mice **scurry** across our kitchen floor.*
3) *The passengers **hastened** to catch the bus.*
4) *She **dashed** inside as it started to rain.*

Opposites: **dally, dawdle**

hurt verb

To **hurt** means to damage someone or something.
*Beth **hurt** her knee when she fell on the ski slope.*

> 1) **bruise** 2) **harm** 3) **injure** 4) **wound**

1) *I **bruised** my leg when I tripped over the log.*
2) *Kelly tried not to **harm** the little mouse.*
3) *If you fall off a horse you could **injure** yourself.*
4) *She **wounded** her finger on the sharp nail.*

idea noun

An **idea** is a thought or plan in your mind.
*It was a good **idea** to go to the beach.*

> 1) **concept** 2) **plan** 3) **theory** 4) **suggestion**

1) *The garden design was the architect's **concept**.*
2) *The prisoners made a **plan** to escape.*
3) *The scientist was sure his **theory** was right.*
4) *The captain's **suggestion** about the game was the best.*

ideal adjective

Something that is **ideal** is just right in every way.
*This spot is the **ideal** place for our picnic.*

> 1) **perfect** 2) **excellent** 3) **faultless** 4) **model**

1) *She found the **perfect** shoes to match her blue dress.*
2) *"That apple pie was an **excellent** dessert!" said Uncle Joe.*
3) *The launch of the space rocket was **faultless**.*
4) *My teacher says that I am a **model** student.*

Opposites: **imperfect, wrong**

ignore verb

To **ignore** something means to pay no attention to it.
*Dad decided to **ignore** the cat's bad behaviour.*

> 1) **disregard** 2) **overlook** 3) **turn a blind eye**

1) *"I cannot **disregard** your past offences,"
said the judge.*
2) *The director **overlooked** all the actor's good work.*
3) *The nurse **turned a blind eye** to the patient's complaints.*

ill adjective

When you are **ill**, you are not well.
*I stayed in bed when I was **ill** with chickenpox.*

> 1) **sick** 2) **unwell** 3) **queasy** 4) **ailing**

1) *I visited my **sick** cousin in the hospital.*
2) *George felt **unwell** after such a big meal.*
3) *She felt **queasy** when she travelled on the boat.*
4) *My **ailing** grandma has to go to the doctor.*

Opposites: **healthy, well**

important adjective

If something is **important**, it is of great value.
*The mayor is an **important** person in our town.*

> 1) **high ranking** 2) **key** 3) **leading** 4) **urgent**

1) *A colonel is a **high-ranking** officer in the army.*
2) *Ben is a **key** player in the basketball team.*
3) *The young actress had a **leading** role in the play.*
4) *Mr King got an **urgent** letter from his lawyer.*

Opposite: **unimportant**

impossible adjective

If something is **impossible**, you cannot do that thing.
*It was **impossible** to open the rusty lock.*

> 1) **hopeless** 2) **out of the question** 3) **unachievable**

1) *Captain Scott's race to the South Pole was a **hopeless** journey.*
2) *A cure for the disease seemed **out of the question**.*
3) *The swimmers felt that setting a new world record was **unachievable**.*

Opposites: **achievable, possible**

incredible adjective

If something is **incredible**, it is hard to believe that it is true.
*The old sailor told us some **incredible** stories.*

> 1) **far-fetched** 2) **implausible** 3) **absurd**

1) *The storyteller told **far-fetched** tales about giants and dragons.*
2) *Her reasons for missing the appointment were **implausible**.*
3) *No one believed the rascal's **absurd** story.*

Opposites: **believable, credible**

insect noun

An **insect** is a small creature with six legs.
*The young plant was covered with **insects**.*

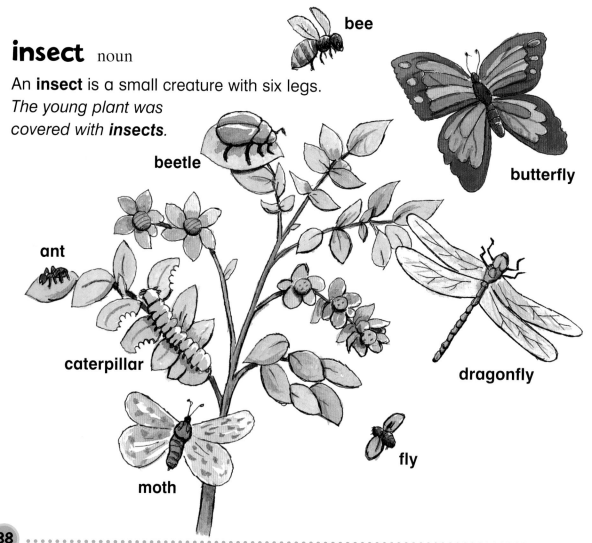

bee

beetle

butterfly

ant

caterpillar

dragonfly

moth

fly

inside adjective

The **inside** of something is the part that you cannot see from the outside.
*The letter was in the **inside** pocket of my coat.*

> 1) **internal** 2) **inner** 3) **interior**

1) The **internal** walls of the house were painted blue.
2) Donna was quiet because she wanted to keep her **inner** feelings to herself.
3) My sister is taking a three-year course in **interior** design.

Opposites: **exterior, outside**

instrument noun

An **instrument** is something you play to make music.
*There are lots of **instruments** in the music room.*

tambourine

guitar

drum

harp

piano

cello

trumpet

trombone

interesting adjective

If something is **interesting**, you want to find out more about it.
*My brother is reading an **interesting** book about dinosaurs.*

> 1) **fascinating** 2) **compelling** 3) **gripping** 4) **intriguing**

1) *Dad thinks model building is a **fascinating** hobby.*
2) *We watched a **compelling** film on Saturday.*
3) *The new play had a **gripping** plot.*
4) *The mystery of the stolen gems was **intriguing**.*

Opposites: **boring, uninteresting**

invisible adjective

If something is **invisible**, you cannot see it.
*The thieves made **invisible** clothes for the Emperor.*

> 1) **concealed** 2) **hidden** 3) **undetectable**

1) *The entrance to the cave was **concealed** behind a rock.*
2) *The chameleon was **hidden** by the leaves of the tree.*
3) *After the operation my scar was **undetectable**.*

Opposite: **visible**

invite verb

To **invite** means to ask someone to do something.
*Beth wanted to **invite** her friends to a sleepover.*

> 1) **ask** 2) **solicit** 3) **call on**

1) *Tony **asked** Nick to stay for the weekend.*
2) *The general **solicited** the opinion of his most loyal soldiers.*
3) *The candidate **called on** his opponent to explain.*

jealous adjective

If you are **jealous** you are angry or upset because someone has something you want.
*Jack was **jealous** of Ted's new bike.*

> 1) **envious** 2) **resentful** 3) **green with envy**

1) *Beth was **envious** of her friend's pretty clothes.*
2) *He was **resentful** about Tom's expensive watch.*
3) *The toddler was **green with envy** because the new baby got so much attention.*

jet noun

A **jet** is a fast stream of liquid or gas that shoots out.
*The elephant shot a **jet** of water over its back.*

> 1) **gush** 2) **spray** 3) **spurt** 4) **fountain**

1) *The burst pipe sent a **gush** of water over the road.*
2) *We used a special **spray** to get rid of the ants.*
3) *A sudden **spurt** of energy helped her to win the race.*
4) *In the middle of the lake was a beautiful **fountain**.*

jewel noun

A **jewel** is a beautiful stone that is worth a lot of money.
*The crown was studded with gleaming **jewels**.*

> 1) **gem** 2) **precious stone** 3) **rock** 4) **gemstone**

1) *The burglar stole **gems** from the jeweller's shop.*
2) *A ruby is a **precious stone**.*
3) *Some people call diamonds **rocks**.*
4) *Mum's gold necklace has three **gemstones** on it.*

Jj job

job noun

A **job** is something you do or something you are paid to do.
*It was Victoria's **job** to pack the books into boxes.*

> 1) **work** 2) **chore** 3) **task** 4) **occupation**

1) *My brother does part-time **work** at a garage.*
2) *The twins have to do their **chores** before they go out to play.*
3) *My first **task** each day is to clean out the rabbit's hutch.*
4) *Chris wants an **occupation** where she can work with animals.*

join verb

To **join** means to bring together.
*The minister **joined** the couple in marriage.*

> 1) **connect** 2) **link** 3) **unite**

1) *The little boy **connected** the two pieces of the jigsaw puzzle.*
2) *The train cars are **linked** together.*
3) *The ranger tried to **unite** the lost cub with its mother.*

Opposite: **separate**

joke verb

To **joke** is to say or do something that makes people laugh.
*Fred likes to **joke** about his wife's cooking.*

> 1) **ridicule** 2) **tease** 3) **mock**

1) *Matthew **ridiculed** his best friend's haircut.*
2) *I **teased** my sister for being afraid of spiders.*
3) *Her stepsisters **mocked** Cinderella's ragged clothes.*

joke noun

A **joke** is a trick or a story that makes people laugh.
*We all giggled at Miranda's **jokes**.*

> 1) **jest** 2) **prank** 3) **gag** 4) **wisecrack**

1) *Martin's **jest** made the teacher laugh.*
2) *Alice played a **prank** on her mum.*
3) *Dad is always telling **gags**.*
4) *Jessie's **wisecracks** hurt my feelings.*

jolt verb

To **jolt** means to move quickly and suddenly.
*The bus driver braked and **jolted** the passengers.*

> 1) **jostle** 2) **jerk** 3) **shake**

1) *The rude man **jostled** his way through the crowd.*
2) *The train **jerked** forward as it set off from the station.*
3) *We could feel all the houses **shake** during
   the earthquake.*

journey noun

When you go on a **journey** you travel somewhere.
*The **journey** to Australia was very long.*

> 1) **trip** 2) **voyage** 3) **expedition** 4) **trek** 5) **excursion**

1) *We are going on an overseas **trip** to Mexico.*
2) *Columbus's first **voyage** to the New World was in 1492.*
3) *Mary told exciting stories about her **expedition** to
   the North Pole.*
4) *The scouts had a long **trek** ahead of them.*
5) *We went on an **excursion** to the famous botanical gardens.*

judge noun

A **judge** is someone who gives a final decision in a court or a game of sport.
*The **judge** sent the burglar to prison.*

> 1) **referee** 2) **umpire** 3) **adjudicator**

1) *The **referee** gave a free kick to the red team.*
2) *The **umpire** watched the tennis match carefully.*
3) *The **adjudicator** made a fair decision.*

judge verb

To **judge** something means to make a decision about it.
*A famous artist was going to **judge** who had done the best painting.*

> 1) **assess** 2) **appraise** 3) **evaluate**

1) *The teacher **assessed** the students' work.*
2) *We tried to **appraise** the new sculptures in the museum.*
3) *The experts **evaluated** the antique furniture.*

jump verb

To **jump** means to leap up into the air.
*Ben's puppy could **jump** very high.*

> 1) **bounce** 2) **hop** 3) **leap** 4) **spring**

1) *Everyone **bounced** on the bouncy castle.*
2) *When Kelly hurt her foot she had to **hop**.*
3) *A leopard can **leap** up into a tree.*
4) *Ben hid in the cupboard so that he could **spring** out on his sister.*

keen adjective

If you are **keen**, you are eager.
*Kevin was **keen** to do well at swimming.*

> 1) **avid** 2) **eager** 3) **enthusiastic** 4) **anxious**

1) *My sister is an **avid** tennis fan.*
2) *The librarian was **eager** to help the trainees.*
3) *Sean was an **enthusiastic** goalkeeper.*
4) *Jane was **anxious** to impress the judges.*

Opposite: **unenthusiastic**

keep verb

To **keep** means to have something and not let go of it.
*We were able to **keep** one of the puppies.*

> 1) **save** 2) **reserve** 3) **retain**

1) *I **save** my change in a big glass jar.*
2) *The dancers **reserved** their best performance for the final show.*
3) *The little girl wanted to **retain** her library books.*

Opposites: **get rid of, release**

kid noun

A **kid** is a young child.
*When I was a **kid** I never ate green vegetables.*

> 1) **child** 2) **baby** 3) **toddler** 4) **youngster**

1) *My little sister is a really mischievous **child**.*
2) *The **baby** would not stop crying.*
3) *The **toddler** could not reach the top shelf.*
4) *The youth club is full of **youngsters**.*

kill verb

If you **kill** a person or an animal, it dies.
*The lion **killed** its prey.*

> 1) **slay** 2) **execute** 3) **murder** 4) **assassinate**

1) *St George had to **slay** the dragon to save the princess.*
2) *The prisoner was **executed** at dawn.*
3) *The police discovered that the victim had been **murdered**.*
4) *The men plotted to **assassinate** the president.*

kind adjective

If you are **kind**, you are gentle and caring.
*She was **kind** to her brother when he hurt himself.*

> 1) **compassionate** 2) **gentle** 3) **loving** 4) **considerate**

1) *The **compassionate** nurse felt sorry for the patient.*
2) *The farmer was very **gentle** with the newborn lamb.*
3) *My grandpa is a very **loving** person.*
4) *It was **considerate** of Fred to send me some flowers.*

Opposites: **cruel, mean, unkind**

kind noun

A **kind** is a sort or a type.
*What **kind** of music do you like?*

> 1) **variety** 2) **breed** 3) **species** 4) **type**

1) *Black Dawn is a new **variety** of tulip.*
2) *Rex was a rare **breed** of dog.*
3) *The explorer found a new **species** of monkey.*
4) *Darjeeling is a **type** of tea.*

kneel verb

To **kneel** is to get down on your knees.
*The prince **kneeled** and asked the princess to marry him.*

> 1) **bend** 2) **bow down** 3) **stoop**

1) *She had to **bend** down to talk to the child.*
2) *The priests **bowed down** in front of the altar.*
3) *Grandpa **stooped** to smell the flowers.*

knock verb

To **knock** means to hit or bang.
*Jack reached up to **knock** on the front door.*

> 1) **hit** 2) **rap** 3) **tap** 4) **bang**

1) *The boy **hit** the ball past the fielders.*
2) *The librarian sometimes has to **rap** on the desk to get our attention.*
3) *The carpenter **tapped** the nail with a hammer.*
4) *Shirley **banged** on the window until we let her in.*

knot verb

If you **knot** something, you tie together two pieces of rope or string.
*The sailor **knotted** the ropes to attach the sails.*

> 1) **tie** 2) **loop** 3) **bind** 4) **secure**

1) *"I can **tie** my shoelaces now!" said Carly.*
2) *Mum **looped** the string around both packages.*
3) *The nurse had to **bind** the cut on my hand with a bandage.*
4) *Ben **secured** his bike to the fence with a bike chain.*

Opposites: **unfasten, untie**

know verb

If you **know** about something, you understand it.
*Dad and Patrick **know** how to put up a tent.*

> 1) **realize** 2) **understand** 3) **see** 4) **be sure of**

1) *The actress didn't **realize** how late she was.*
2) *The children **understood** why their mum was so annoyed with them.*
3) *She could **see** why her maths homework was wrong.*
4) *The angry customer **was sure of** his facts.*

know verb

If you **know** someone, you recognize that person.
*Tom **knew** all the people at his birthday party.*

> 1) **identify** 2) **recognize** 3) **remember**

1) *The woman told the police that she could **identify** the thief.*
2) *Although the sisters had not met for 20 years, they **recognized** each other instantly.*
3) *Jason **remembered** all his friends from his old club.*

knowledge noun

If you have **knowledge** about something, you know facts about it.
*All the contestants had good general **knowledge**.*

> 1) **experience** 2) **understanding** 3) **grasp**

1) *The mountaineer had a wealth of **experience**.*
2) *The researcher's **understanding** of the disease was excellent.*
3) *The new recruits wanted to **grasp** how to sail a boat.*

Opposite: **ignorance**

land noun

Land is the solid earth under your feet.
*The rich man owned lots of **land**.*

> 1) **ground** 2) **soil** 3) **earth**

1) *The **ground** was too hard to dig.*
2) *The farmer ploughs the **soil** with his new tractor.*
3) *Crops grow well in good **earth**.*

land verb

To **land** means to stop travelling and come to rest on land or water.
*The helicopter **landed** on the hotel roof.*

> 1) **touch down** 2) **arrive** 3) **alight**

1) *The plane **touched down** on the runway.*
2) *The boat **arrived** at a desert island.*
3) *A wasp **alighted** on the soldier's nose.*

Opposite: **take off**

large adjective

If something is **large** it is very big.
*My aunt received a **large** package in the post.*

> 1) **big** 2) **massive** 3) **colossal** 4) **enormous**

1) *A toucan has a **big**, colourful beak.*
2) *The weightlifter has **massive** shoulders.*
3) *We looked up at the **colossal** building.*
4) *The giant had a pair of **enormous** feet!*

Opposites: **little, small, tiny**

last adjective

If something is **last**, it is the final one.
*The letter z is the **last** letter of the alphabet.*

> 1) **closing** 2) **final** 3) **concluding**

1) *A goal was scored in the **closing** minute of the game.*
2) *The penalty shoot-out was the **final** chance to win the match.*
3) *The **concluding** episode of the film was very exciting.*

Opposites: **first, initial, opening**

last verb

If something **lasts**, it stays in place.
*A stone house is built to **last**.*

> 1) **endure** 2) **continue** 3) **persist**

1) *Shakespeare's work has **endured** long after his death.*
2) *Isabel wanted the music to **continue** forever.*
3) *The tropical rain **persisted** for three days.*

late adjective

If you are **late**, you arrive after the agreed time.
*Jenny was **late** for swimming practice.*

> 1) **behind** 2) **delayed** 3) **overdue** 4) **belated**

1) *I am **behind** with my school project.*
2) *The **delayed** train arrived two hours later.*
3) *My books are **overdue** at the library.*
4) *I received a **belated** Christmas present in January.*

Opposites: **early, on time**

laugh verb

When you **laugh**, you make a happy sound because something is funny.
*People always **laugh** at my uncle's jokes.*

> 1) **chuckle** 2) **giggle** 3) **guffaw** 4) **chortle**

1) *We started to **chuckle** when we saw the little pink monster on TV.*
2) *I could not stop **giggling** when I heard the funny story.*
3) *The ridiculous story made us **guffaw**.*
4) *Everyone **chortled** at the funny play.*

Opposites: **cry, sob, weep**

layer noun

A **layer** is something flat that sits above or below a surface.
*The ground was covered with a **layer** of snow.*

> 1) **coating** 2) **film** 3) **sheet**

1) *The cake had a **coating** of white icing.*
2) *There was a **film** of dust over the furniture.*
3) *The car skidded on a **sheet** of ice.*

lazy adjective

If you are **lazy**, you do not want to do any work.
*Jack was a **lazy** boy who stayed in bed all day.*

> 1) **idle** 2) **slothful** 3) **careless** 4) **indolent**

1) *Sarah was **idle** and did not go outside to play.*
2) *The **slothful** boy never straightened his bedroom.*
3) *The store's employees had a very **careless** way of working.*
4) *The **indolent** waitress was always sitting down.*

Opposites: **active, busy, energetic**

lead verb

To **lead** means to show someone the way.
*The guide has to **lead** the tourists past the ruins.*

> 1) **guide** 2) **conduct** 3) **escort** 4) **usher**

1) *She **guided** the blind man across the street.*
2) *The waiter **conducted** us to our table.*
3) *Charlotte **escorted** her parents to their seats.*
4) *The manager **ushered** us into the dining room.*

Opposite: **follow**

leave verb

When you **leave**, you go away.
*When I **leave** home I'm going to take my cat with me.*

> 1) **go** 2) **depart** 3) **make tracks** 4) **set out**

1) *We have to **go** to our tent before it gets dark.*
2) *We planned to **depart** at six o'clock.*
3) *Towards the end of the party the guests began to **make tracks** for home.*
4) *I **set out** for school straight after breakfast.*

Opposites: **arrive, come**

lie verb

To **lie** means to rest in a flat position.
*Mum went to **lie** down after lunch.*

> 1) **be recumbent** 2) **recline** 3) **lounge**

1) *The princess **was recumbent** on a velvet couch.*
2) *Jasmine **reclined** on her bed.*
3) *My brother likes to **lounge** on the sofa.*

Opposite: **stand**

light adjective

If something is **light** it does not weigh very much and is easy to carry.
*The small bag was **light** enough to carry onto the plane.*

> 1) **flimsy**   2) **lightweight**   3) **slight**

1) *She wore a **flimsy** dress because it was such a hot day.*
2) *A feather is **lightweight** when compared to a bone.*
3) *My younger cousin is small and **slight**.*

Opposite: **heavy**

light noun

A **light** is an object that shines and makes the
area around it bright.
*You turn on the **light** when you walk into a dark hall.*

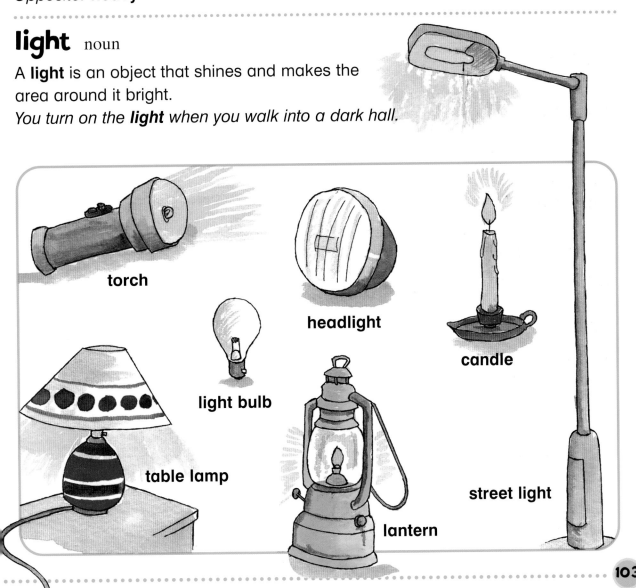

torch

headlight

candle

light bulb

table lamp

lantern

street light

Ll like

like verb

If you **like** something, you are pleased with it.
"I like this sweater best," said Lauren.

> 1) **admire** 2) **enjoy** 3) **be fond of**

1) *The jeweller **admired** the new silver brooch.*
2) *Grandma **enjoys** baking cakes.*
3) *Anna **is fond of** her next-door neighbour.*

Opposites: **dislike, hate**

like adjective

If one thing is **like** another, it is the same or similar.
*Mum's new car was **like** her old one.*

> 1) **identical to** 2) **comparable to** 3) **similar to**

1) *Lisa's outfit was **identical to** her twin sister's.*
2) *The professor's discoveries are **comparable to** mine.*
3) *My brother looks **similar to** me.*

Opposites: **unlike, dissimilar to**

litter noun

Litter is rubbish that people throw on the ground.
*There was **litter** all over our street.*

> 1) **rubbish** 2) **refuse** 3) **waste** 4) **debris**

1) *You should always throw your **rubbish** in the bin.*
2) *Our **refuse** is collected every Thursday.*
3) *The **waste** from the steel factory goes into the local river.*
4) ***Debris** from the sunken ship floated to the surface.*

little adjective

If something is **little** it is small or tiny.
*The toddler was too **little** to go on the Big Dipper.*

> 1) **small** 2) **miniature** 3) **minute** 4) **tiny**

1) *We planted a **small** tree in the garden.*
2) *My grandma collects **miniature** teapots.*
3) *The **minute** beetle crept through the keyhole.*
4) *The baby wore **tiny** mittens on her hands.*

Opposites: **big, large**

lonely adjective

If you are **lonely** you feel sad because you are alone.
*Jamal was **lonely** when all his friends went home.*

> 1) **friendless** 2) **alone** 3) **solitary** 4) **forsaken**

1) *The **friendless** boy sat at a desk by himself.*
2) *The old lady lived **alone** in a big house.*
3) *The artist was a **solitary** man.*
4) *The puppy felt **forsaken** when its owner went away.*

long adjective

If something is **long** it lasts for more time than usual.
*It was a **long** trip to the seashore.*

> 1) **endless** 2) **lengthy** 3) **extended**

1) *The **endless** lecture was very boring.*
2) *The teacher gave a **lengthy** explanation about the Solar System.*
3) *I took an **extended** holiday in Australia.*

Opposite: **short**

Beach
25 miles

long for verb

To **long for** something means to wish for it strongly.
*The children **longed for** their maths class to end.*

1) **yearn** 2) **crave** 3) **hunger** 4) **desire**

1) *The immigrant **yearned** to go back home.*
2) *He **craved** all the cakes and pastries he saw.*
3) *They **hungered** for some more interesting books.*
4) *The astronauts **desired** to return to Earth.*

look verb

To **look** means to turn your eyes towards
someone or something.
*Jack went to **look** at the new house.*

1) **examine** 2) **gaze** 3) **stare** 4) **watch**

1) *The doctor had to **examine** the wound.*
2) *The artist **gazed** at the beautiful painting.*
3) *Dan knew it was rude to **stare** at people.*
4) *I **watched** the bird through my binoculars.*

lose verb

If you **lose** something, you cannot find it.
*"Put the money in your purse so you don't **lose** it!" said Mum.*

1) **misplace** 2) **mislay** 3) **drop**

1) *Jenny **misplaced** her textbook and had to buy a new one.*
2) *Dad **mislays** his car keys all the time.*
3) *The baby has **dropped** her doll somewhere in the house.*

Opposite: **find**

loud adjective

If something is **loud**, it is very noisy.
The plate fell to the floor with a loud crash.

> 1) **blaring** 2) **deafening** 3) **noisy** 4) **thunderous**

1) The **blaring** music disturbed everyone.
2) A pneumatic drill makes a **deafening** noise.
3) The **noisy** mob stormed through the streets.
4) Uncle Jed has a **thunderous** voice.

Opposites: **low, quiet, soft**

love verb

If you **love** someone or something, that person or thing
means a lot to you.
Daniel loves his parents very much.

> 1) **adore** 2) **worship** 3) **dote on**

1) I **adore** my new kitten.
2) The small boy **worships** his older brother.
3) Professor Williams **doted on** his students.

Opposite: **hate**

lovely adjective

If something is **lovely**, it is delightful or pretty.
The bride is wearing a lovely silk dress.

> 1) **attractive** 2) **beautiful** 3) **exquisite**

1) The model wore an **attractive** hat.
2) **Beautiful** flowers grow in the garden.
3) My sister has some **exquisite** jewellery.

Opposites: **hideous, ugly**

machine noun

A **machine** is a piece of equipment with parts that work together to do a special job.
*A washing **machine** cleans clothes.*

> 1) **device** 2) **apparatus** 3) **tool**

1) *Professor Sparks invented a **device** for cleaning his house.*
2) *Their **apparatus** was kept in the laboratory.*
3) *Dad has a special **tool** for cleaning out the gutters.*

mad adjective

If you are **mad**, you are very angry.
*The **mad** bull charged at the farmer.*

> 1) **furious** 2) **irate** 3) **raging** 4) **seething**

1) *The athlete was **furious** when he lost the race.*
2) *Our dog was **irate** when the cat ate his food.*
3) *The **raging** pirate jumped off his ship into the ocean.*
4) *The grumpy old man was **seething** with anger.*

magic noun

Magic is the use of spells to do clever things.
*The wizard used **magic** to wash his dishes.*

> 1) **sorcery** 2) **witchcraft** 3) **wizardry**

1) *The puppet was brought to life by **sorcery**.*
2) *Polly wanted to learn about **witchcraft**.*
3) *"My **wizardry** will turn you into a frog,"*
   cackled the wizard.

main adjective

Main means the most important.
*I played the **main** character in the school play.*

1) **chief** 2) **principal** 3) **prime** 4) **head**

1) *"The **chief** problem is the leaking roof," said the builder.*
2) *The **principal** ballerina is very tall.*
3) *Roger the Robber is our **prime** suspect.*
4) *The **head** officer on board a ship is called a captain.*

Opposite: **minor**

make verb

To **make** means to force a person or an object to do something.
*"Don't **make** me go to the haunted house!" squealed Rosie.*

1) **compel** 2) **force** 3) **oblige**

1) *The rain **compelled** me to put up my umbrella.*
2) *Sam's brother **forced** him to tell lies.*
3) *"Don't **oblige** me to separate you," warned the teacher.*

make verb

When you **make** something, you build it or put it together.
*Mum asked Sarah to **make** dinner.*

1) **create** 2) **build** 3) **produce**

1) *It is fun to **create** colourful pots with clay.*
2) *"I want to **build** a sand castle," said Tim.*
3) *The big factory **produces** cars.*

Opposite: **destroy**

many adjective

Many means a large number of something.
*Tim had **many** friends at his new school.*

> 1) **abundant** 2) **countless** 3) **numerous** 4) **a lot of**

1) *"We have an **abundant** crop of sweetcorn this year," said the farmer.*
2) *Joe made **countless** trips to the sweet shop.*
3) *The class read **numerous** books about space.*
4) *There were **a lot of** skateboards for sale.*

Opposite: **few**

march verb

To **march** is to walk with quick steps like a soldier.
*The battalion of soldiers **marched** across the parade ground.*

> 1) **stride** 2) **parade** 3) **file** 4) **troop**

1) *After a while the walkers at the front began to **stride** out.*
2) *The new cadets will **parade** in front of their general.*
3) *The prisoners **filed** out of their cells.*
4) *When they heard the fire alarm, the audience **trooped** out of the theatre.*

mark noun

A **mark** is a dirty spot.
*I scrubbed the oily **marks** off my jeans.*

> 1) **stain** 2) **smudge** 3) **spot** 4) **smear**

1) *The **stain** would not come out of her evening gown.*
2) *The artist made a **smudge** on his drawing.*
3) *I have a **spot** on my silk tie.*
4) *We found a large **smear** on the window.*

match noun

A **match** is an event in which two people,
or two teams, play against each other.
*The whole family watched the **match** on TV.*

> 1) **competition** 2) **contest** 3) **game**

1) *We cheered when our team won
   the **competition**.*
2) *She challenged me to a skipping **contest**.*
3) *The board **game** lasted for hours.*

matter noun

A **matter** is a subject or business that you need to think about or act upon.
*"We should talk about this **matter**," said the doctor.*

> 1) **issue** 2) **topic** 3) **subject**

1) *The most important **issue** was the increase in nuclear power.*
2) *Our school held a debate on the **topic** of recycling.*
3) *Martin is passionate about the **subject** of politics.*

meal noun

A **meal** is the food that you sit down to eat at different times of the day.
*"Breakfast is my favourite **meal** of the day," said Mum.*

> 1) **feast** 2) **snack** 3) **banquet**

1) *A delicious **feast** was spread
   out on the blanket.*
2) *We had a quick **snack** on
   our way to the airport.*
3) *The king held a
   banquet for his guests.*

mean adjective

If you are **mean**, you are unkind to others.
*Mum told me not to be **mean** to my little sister.*

> 1) **nasty** 2) **unfriendly** 3) **cruel** 4) **selfish**

1) *A bully at school was really **nasty** to me today.*
2) *Stay away from that dog – it looks **unfriendly**.*
3) *We should never be **cruel** to animals.*
4) *Thomas was **selfish** and wouldn't share his toys.*

Opposites: **kind, friendly, generous**

mean verb

What someone or something **means** is what that person
or thing is trying to tell you.
*"I don't understand what you **mean**," said the student.*

> 1) **imply** 2) **indicate** 3) **signify**

1) *His smile **implied** that he was joking.*
2) *A red light **indicates** that you cannot cross the street.*
3) *Dark clouds **signify** that it is going to rain.*

meet verb

To **meet** is to come together.
*"Let's **meet** at the cinema," suggested Annie.*

> 1) **assemble** 2) **gather** 3) **congregate**

1) *The crowd **assembled** outside the town hall.*
2) *We **gather** in the playground every morning.*
3) *Maisy's friends **congregated** in front of her house.*

melt verb

To **melt** is to change to a liquid when heated.
*When the sun came out, the snowman began to **melt**.*

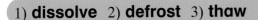
1) **dissolve** 2) **defrost** 3) **thaw**

1) *When you add sugar to tea it **dissolves**.*
2) *I **defrost** my dinner in the microwave.*
3) *Ice **thaws** when the sun shines.*

Opposites: **freeze, harden**

mend verb

To **mend** something means to repair it.
*Matthew tried to **mend** his punctured tyre.*

1) **repair** 2) **darn** 3) **fix**

1) *The builders **repaired** the hole in the roof.*
2) *Aunt Ethel always **darns** her husband's socks.*
3) *"I've **fixed** the motorcycle!" grinned the new mechanic.*

Opposite: **break**

mess noun

A **mess** is an untidy confusion of things.
*"Clean up this **mess**!" yelled Mum.*

1) **chaos** 2) **shambles** 3) **jumble** 4) **clutter**

1) *The room was in **chaos** after the party.*
2) *"My desk is a **shambles**," cried May.*
3) *We helped sort out the **jumble** of clothes.*
4) *The kitchen table was buried under the **clutter**.*

Opposites: **order, tidiness**

metal noun

A **metal** is a hard material that can be used to make many things.
Our knives and forks are made of **metal**.

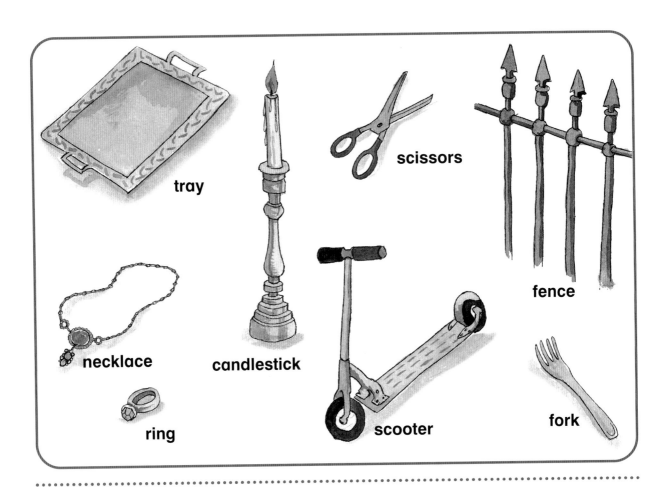

tray

scissors

fence

necklace

candlestick

ring

scooter

fork

middle noun

The **middle** is the point that is halfway between two other points.
White lines are painted down the **middle** *of the road.*

1) **centre** 2) **core** 3) **heart**

1) *I never eat the pips at the* **centre** *of my apple.*
2) *It is very hot at Earth's* **core**.
3) *The statue stands in the* **heart** *of our city.*

mild adjective

If something is **mild**, it is gentle.
*There was a **mild** breeze as we sailed out to sea.*

> 1) **gentle** 2) **serene** 3) **pleasant**

1) *Annabelle is a very **gentle** person.*
2) *Our horse has a **serene** temperament.*
3) *"We had **pleasant** weather on our holiday,"
   smiled George.*

mind noun

Your **mind** is the part of you that lets you think, feel, remember and understand.
*Jake's clever **mind** soon figured out the puzzle.*

> 1) **brain** 2) **intellect** 3) **intelligence**

1) *My **brain** was tired after a day of studying!*
2) *"Use your **intellect** to answer the question," said Mr Mason.*
3) *Everyone admired the smart child's sharp **intelligence**.*

miss verb

If you **miss** someone, you are sad because that person
is no longer with you.
*Carl **missed** the mountains when he went to live in the city.*

> 1) **pine** 2) **long for** 3) **want**

1) *The dog **pined** for its owners when they went away.*
2) *When I moved school I **longed for** my old friends.*
3) *Mark was homesick and **wanted** his mum.*

miss verb

If you **miss**, you fail to find or hit a target.
*We all groaned when the goalkeeper **missed** the ball.*

1) **avoid** 2) **evade** 3) **dodge**

1) *We left early to **avoid** the rush hour.*
2) *The crafty jewel thief **evaded** the police.*
3) *"No one is going to **dodge** Sports Day!"
   shouted the sports teacher.*

Opposites: **find, hit**

mistake noun

A **mistake** is something that you do wrong, or the wrong thing.
*I made lots of **mistakes** in my spelling test.*

1) **blunder** 2) **error** 3) **oversight**

1) *The clumsy man apologised for his **blunder**.*
2) *"I made an **error** when I trusted you," snapped the supervisor.*
3) *We missed the last train because of an **oversight**.*

mix verb

To **mix** means to put together.
*Mum had to **mix** the ingredients for my birthday cake.*

1) **blend** 2) **combine** 3) **mingle** 4) **merge**

1) *The painter **blended** the colours carefully.*
2) *You **combine** eggs with milk to make an omelette.*
3) *The funny clown **mingled** with the audience.*
4) *All the classes **merged** for a dancing lesson.*

Opposite: **separate**

moan noun

A **moan** is an unhappy sound that shows you are in pain or in trouble.
*The patient gave a **moan** as the doctor felt his stomach.*

1) **groan** 2) **wail** 3) **sob** 4) **whine**

1) *We heard a **groan** coming from the cupboard.*
2) *I let out a **wail** when I saw the ghost!*
3) *My sister's loud **sob** woke me up.*
4) *The dog's **whine** was a horrible noise.*

modern adjective

If something is **modern** it is up to date.
*My dad hates **modern** music.*

1) **latest** 2) **contemporary** 3) **fashionable** 4) **current**

1) *"I only wear the **latest** clothes," said the model.*
2) *The **contemporary** furniture looked odd in the old house.*
3) *My aunt wears very **fashionable** shoes.*
4) *I like to read books by **current** writers.*

Opposites: **dated, old-fashioned**

money noun

Money is the notes and coins you use to buy things.
*I earn extra **money** by delivering newspapers.*

1) **cash** 2) **change** 3) **funds** 4) **riches**

1) *Dad gave me some **cash** to buy new trainers.*
2) *"Have you got any **change** for the vending machine?" Kathy asked.*
3) *He saved up his **funds** to buy a new car.*
4) *All the king's **riches** couldn't buy him what he wanted.*

monster noun

A **monster** is an imaginary beast.
*I read about **monsters**
in fairy tales.*

giant

dragon

beast

werewolf

goblin

ogre

troll

move verb

To **move** is to change the place or position of something.
"Move your feet closer together!" cried the gym coach.

> 1) **carry** 2) **push** 3) **transfer**

1) *The men **carry** the sofa down the stairs.*
2) *"**Push** those boxes out of the way!" said Dad.*
3) *I **transferred** the heavy bag to my other hand.*

mumble verb

To **mumble** is to speak unclearly in a quiet voice.
*"Speak up! I can't hear you when you **mumble**," said Grandpa.*

> 1) **murmur** 2) **mutter** 3) **whisper**

1) *She heard some people **murmur** behind her in the lift.*
2) *David **muttered** angrily to himself when he tripped on his shoelaces.*
3) *"Help me!" **whispered** the injured soldier.*

mystery noun

A **mystery** is something puzzling that you cannot explain.
*The detective was working on a strange **mystery**.*

> 1) **puzzle** 2) **riddle** 3) **enigma**

1) *A smart girl solved the **puzzle** of Grace's missing glasses.*
2) *"I love a good **riddle**," chuckled my uncle.*
3) *Where the new science teacher had come from was an **enigma**.*

narrow adjective

If something is **narrow**, it is small in width.
*The man walked down the **narrow** street.*

1) **thin** 2) **slender** 3) **slim**

1) *Canal boats are long and **thin**.*
2) *The model had a **slender** waist.*
3) *We squeezed through the **slim** space in the fence.*

Opposites: **broad, wide**

nasty adjective

To be **nasty** means to be very unpleasant.
*The **nasty** girl hit her little brother.*

1) **spiteful** 2) **unkind** 3) **vile** 4) **vicious**

1) *Richard is a **spiteful** boy.*
2) *"Don't be so **unkind**," said Archie.*
3) *My **vile** cousin always pulls my hair.*
4) *Martha had a **vicious** temper.*

Opposite: **nice**

naughty adjective

To be **naughty** means to behave badly.
*The **naughty** twins tired out their babysitter.*

1) **disobedient** 2) **bad** 3) **impish**

1) *Ted was **disobedient** and broke the rules.*
2) *"**Bad** dog!" said Dad when he saw the mess.*
3) *The **impish** child was always in trouble.*

Opposites: **good, polite, well-behaved**

near preposition

Near means close to something.
*"I love living **near** the sea," said the old sailor.*

1) **adjacent** 2) **beside** 3) **close** 4) **neighbouring**

1) *The two houses had **adjacent** front doors.*
2) *Our house is **beside** a stream.*
3) *Jenny lived **close** to her best friend.*
4) *Henry threw rubbish into the **neighbouring** garden.*

Opposites: **distant, far**

neat adjective

To be **neat** means to be tidy.
*Pat has very **neat** handwriting.*

1) **tidy** 2) **orderly** 3) **trim**

1) *David liked to keep his room **tidy**.*
2) *"It is important to be **orderly**,"*
   said the captain.
3) *Laura looked wonderful in her **trim** suit.*

Opposite: **messy, untidy**

need verb

To **need** means to want something urgently.
*"I **need** more fruit," said Mum.*

1) **crave** 2) **require** 3) **want**

1) *"I **crave** some chocolate," sighed Helen.*
2) *To make a greetings card you **require** paper, a pencil*
   and some paints.
3) *Ted and Ravi **want** spaghetti for dinner.*

nervous adjective

To be **nervous** is to be easily scared or worried.
*Sarah felt **nervous** when she saw the big dog.*

> 1) **anxious** 2) **uneasy** 3) **timid** 4) **edgy**

1) *Alice was **anxious** about her science test.*
2) *Grandma was **uneasy** about flying in a plane.*
3) *Mice are **timid** creatures.*
4) *I got **edgy** when I heard the door creak open.*

Opposites: **calm, relaxed**

new adjective

If something is **new** it has just been made, thought of or bought.
*Aunt Jesse bought a **new** hat for Easter.*

> 1) **fresh** 2) **original** 3) **novel**

1) *The teacher asked for some **fresh** ideas.*
2) *We saw an **original** play at the new theatre.*
3) *Norman has a **novel** diet plan.*

Opposite: **old**

next adjective

The **next** is the one that comes
right after.
*We waited to catch the **next** bus.*

> 1) **subsequent** 2) **following** 3) **later**

1) *"I'll take the **subsequent** train," said Jack.*
2) *The circus arrived the **following** day.*
3) *They went to the **later** showing at the cinema.*

Opposite: **previous**

nice adjective

Something that is **nice** is pleasing.
*Daisy had a **nice**, relaxing afternoon.*

> 1) **pleasant** 2) **agreeable** 3) **charming**

1) *The house had a **pleasant** garden.*
2) *Lucy's new boyfriend was very **agreeable**.*
3) *The **charming** boy shook hands with the visitor.*

Opposites: **nasty, horrid, unpleasant**

noisy adjective

If something is **noisy** it is too loud.
*The **noisy** dog wouldn't stop barking.*

> 1) **deafening** 2) **loud** 3) **strident** 4) **piercing**

1) *The music at the disco was **deafening**.*
2) *The jet's engines made a **loud** noise as the plane took off.*
3) *"You've got a very **strident** voice," said the nurse.*
4) *Shelley let out a **piercing** scream.*

Opposites: **quiet**

nonsense noun

Words, actions or ideas that are **nonsense** are silly or have no meaning.
*Mr Lewin said that Robert's story was a lot of **nonsense**.*

> 1) **gibberish** 2) **drivel** 3) **silliness**

1) *The madman was talking **gibberish**.*
2) *"You're talking **drivel**," snapped the captain.*
3) *"Stop this **silliness**," ordered our maths teacher.*

Opposite: **sense**

normal adjective

If something is **normal**, it is usual and what you would expect.
*The school bus left at the **normal** time.*

> 1) **usual** 2) **ordinary** 3) **regular** 4) **average**

1) The **usual** driver was taking a sick day.
2) The magician held up an **ordinary** cap.
3) I bought a **regular**-size milkshake.
4) "He's an **average** student," said the music teacher.

Opposites: **strange, abnormal**

nosy adjective

To be **nosy** is to snoop or interfere.
***Nosy** Norma was always peeking through keyholes.*

> 1) **inquisitive** 2) **prying** 3) **snooping**

1) "Don't be so **inquisitive**," grinned Dad.
2) I hid my designs away from **prying** eyes.
3) The **snooping** detective found all the clues
   he needed.

Opposite: **uninterested**

nothing noun

Nothing is the absence of something.
*Donald had **nothing** to do.*

> 1) **emptiness** 2) **zero** 3) **blank**

1) There was **emptiness** where my bike should have been.
2) The temperature fell to **zero** overnight.
3) I tried to remember her name, but my mind was a **blank**.

Opposite: **something**

notice noun

A **notice** is a sign that gives information.
*The teacher pinned a **notice** on the bulletin board.*

> 1) **advertisement** 2) **sign** 3) **poster**

1) *We put an **advertisement** in the newspaper.*
2) *The **sign** said 'Closed For Repairs'.*
3) *The **poster** says that the circus is coming next week.*

notice verb

To **notice** is to see or observe.
*Eileen **noticed** that her garden was flooded.*

> 1) **spot** 2) **observe** 3) **detect**

1) *"Did you **spot** me on TV?" asked William.*
2) *Oliver **observed** a rare bird in the garden.*
3) *We all **detected** a strange smell.*

Opposite: **miss**

nuisance noun

A **nuisance** is something or someone that is annoying.
*My little sister is a terrible **nuisance**.*

> 1) **pain** 2) **pest** 3) **irritation**

1) *It was a **pain** to have to go out in the rain.*
2) *"Don't be such a **pest**!" yelled my brother.*
3) *The sound of drilling in the street is
   a big **irritation**.*

Oo obedient

obedient adjective

If you are **obedient**, you do as you are told.
*The **obedient** dog came to his owner when she called.*

1) **dutiful** 2) **submissive** 3) **respectful**

1) *The **dutiful** daughter looked after her parents.*
2) *Jeff is a **submissive** person.*
3) *The **respectful** servant bowed to the king.*

Opposites: **disobedient, rebellious**

object noun

The **object** is the main purpose or target.
*The **object** of a football game is to score lots of goals.*

1) **aim** 2) **goal** 3) **purpose**

1) *Jim's **aim** in life was to become very rich!*
2) *Mum's **goal** was to clean the whole house.*
3) *The **purpose** of going to the market was to buy some fruit.*

object noun

An **object** is a thing you can touch and see.
*We had to guess what the **object** was with our eyes closed.*

1) **article** 2) **thing** 3) **item**

1) *Maureen held the strange **article** in her hand.*
2) *The new computer was a tiny **thing**.*
3) *There were five **items** in my purse.*

odd adjective

If something is **odd**, it is different or unusual.
*Dad had an **odd** expression on his face.*

1) **weird** 2) **bizarre** 3) **peculiar** 4) **strange**

1) *Andrea dyed her hair a **weird** colour.*
2) *"What a **bizarre** boat!" exclaimed the sailor.*
3) *Jane's **peculiar** accent was hard to understand.*
4) *A **strange** noise came from the cupboard.*

Opposite: **normal**

often adverb

Often means frequently.
*Jason **often** visited the zoo.*

1) **frequently** 2) **much** 3) **repeatedly**

1) *The buses to town run **frequently**.*
2) *Shakespeare is a **much**-quoted writer.*
3) *Dave recited the poem **repeatedly**.*

Opposites: **rarely, seldom**

old adjective

If something is **old**, it has existed for a long time.
*Mum wore **old** jeans for gardening.*

1) **aged** 2) **ancient** 3) **elderly**

1) *The **aged** wizard had a long white beard.*
2) *There is an **ancient** table in the living room.*
3) *My grandma is an **elderly** lady.*

Opposites: **new, young**

Oo old

old adjective

If something is **old**, it is the one that came before.
*Our **old** house had five bedrooms.*

> 1) **earlier** 2) **former** 3) **previous**

1) *"This camera is better than the **earlier** model,"*
   grinned Ron.
2) *Andy's **former** job was driving steamrollers.*
3) *My **previous** teacher was very kind.*

Opposites: **current, present**

once adverb

Once means at one time in the past.
*I **once** ran a mile in five minutes.*

> 1) **formerly** 2) **previously** 3) **at one time**

1) *Mrs Evans was **formerly** a nurse.*
2) *Our house was **previously** a monastery.*
3) ***At one time**, dinosaurs roamed the planet.*

only adjective

If something is **only** it is a single one.
*Dan was an **only** child.*

> 1) **lone** 2) **sole** 3) **single**

1) *She was the **lone** girl in the swimming team.*
2) *"Football is my **sole** interest," said Gary.*
3) *The waiter was the **single** witness to the crime.*

only adverb

Only means nothing more than.
*There were **only** three crisps left in the bag.*

> 1) **just** 2) **merely** 3) **totally**

1) *We had **just** 30 seconds to answer the question.*
2) *"You're **merely** a child," said the nasty man.*
3) *"That story is **totally** made up," said the reporter.*

open verb

To **open** means to move or change from a
closed position.
*Many shops **open** at nine o'clock in the morning.*

> 1) **unwrap** 2) **unfasten** 3) **uncork**

1) *Maya quickly **unwrapped** her presents.*
2) *The burglar **unfastened** the window.*
3) *Uncle Bert said he would **uncork** the
   bottle of wine.*

Opposites: **close, shut**

open adjective

If something is **open** it is not closed or locked.
*"The circus is **open**!" cried the clowns.*

> 1) **ajar** 2) **unlocked** 3) **gaping**

1) *My bedroom door was **ajar**.*
2) *The toy cupboard was **unlocked**.*
3) *The dentist looked into my
   gaping mouth.*

OPEN

order verb

To **order** means to command.
*Sergeant Brown **ordered** his soldiers to salute.*

> 1) **command** 2) **direct** 3) **charge** 4) **instruct**

1) *The queen **commanded** everyone to kneel.*
2) *The captain **directed** his crew to abandon ship.*
3) *"I **charge** you to tell the truth!" yelled the judge.*
4) *Mum **instructed** the delivery men to put the bed upstairs.*

ordinary adjective

If something is **ordinary** it is normal or not unexpected.
*Mary wore an **ordinary** coat.*

> 1) **everyday** 2) **normal** 3) **usual** 4) **standard**

1) *A cold is an **everyday** illness.*
2) *The patient's temperature was **normal**.*
3) *I finished school at the **usual** time today.*
4) *White is the **standard** colour for a dishwasher.*

Opposites: **extraordinary, unusual**

organize verb

To **organize** means to plan something
and work out the details.
*I **organized** the school disco.*

> 1) **arrange** 2) **coordinate** 3) **run**

1) *Uncle Bruno **arranged** a surprise party.*
2) *The police **coordinated** a search of a wide area.*
3) *Miss Block **runs** the local marathon every year.*

out adjective

If you are **out**, you are not at home.
*I went to see my best friend but she was **out**.*

> 1) **absent** 2) **away** 3) **elsewhere**

1) *Natalie was **absent** from school on Monday.*
2) *The gardener went **away** for two weeks.*
3) *Jake's mum said he was **elsewhere** with his brother.*

Opposites: **here, in, present**

outside adjective

If something is **outside**, it is away from the inside.
*Dad turned on the **outside** tap.*

> 1) **exterior** 2) **outdoor** 3) **external**

1) *The **exterior** wall was painted white.*
2) *Mum said football was an **outdoor** game.*
3) *The **external** side of the door is scratched.*

Opposite: **inside**

over adjective

If something is **over**, it is in the past.
*We got up when the film was **over**.*

> 1) **finished** 2) **completed** 3) **ended**

1) *We will celebrate when our final exam is **finished**.*
2) *"Is the test **completed**?" asked the scientist.*
3) *When the teacher came in our fun was **ended**.*

painful adjective

If something is **painful**, it hurts.
*Jason had a really **painful** knee.*

> 1) **aching** 2) **sore** 3) **stinging** 4) **throbbing**

1) *The young athlete's legs were **aching**.*
2) *The skier's bruises were very **sore**.*
3) *The child rubbed her **stinging** eyes.*
4) *"I've got a **throbbing** headache," Bella complained.*

Opposite: **painless**

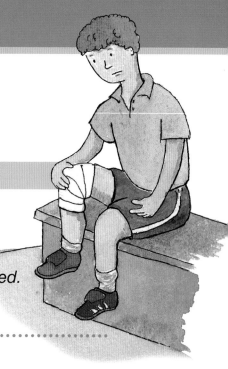

pale adjective

If something is **pale**, it has little or no colour.
*The patient had a **pale** face because she was so ill.*

> 1) **ashen** 2) **colourless** 3) **white**

1) *Her face went **ashen** when she heard the bad news.*
2) *The dying plant's leaves were **colourless**.*
3) *The summer sky was **white** with clouds.*

Opposite: **ruddy**

part noun

A **part** is a section of a whole thing.
*I could only see a **part** of the stage.*

> 1) **piece** 2) **portion** 3) **segment** 4) **fragment**

1) *"Have another **piece** of pizza," said Uncle Roy.*
2) *Marcus saved a **portion** of pie for his brother.*
3) *We shared the **segments** of the orange.*
4) *Only a **fragment** of the original letter from Captain Cook was left.*

pass   verb

To **pass** means to move by something.
*I always **pass** the church on my way to school.*

> 1) **go by**   2) **outdo**   3) **outstrip**

1) *I was scared to **go by** the old haunted house.*
2) *I'd like to **outdo** my best score at netball.*
3) *Zoe **outstripped** all her friends in the hurdles race.*

pass   verb

To **pass** means to transfer or exchange an item.
*Jack **passed** the book to his teacher.*

> 1) **give**   2) **hand**   3) **transfer**

1) *"**Give** me that pencil," said Jennifer rudely.*
2) *We **handed** the fossil around the class.*
3) *I **transferred** the problem to my parents.*

patient   adjective

If you are **patient**, you do not mind having to wait.
*Miss Brown was **patient** with me when I couldn't do the maths problem.*

> 1) **calm**   2) **long-suffering**   3) **untiring**   4) **uncomplaining**

1) *The builder was **calm** when the big beam fell on his foot.*
2) *My **long-suffering** friend always forgives me for being late.*
3) *Marie's work on the difficult problem is **untiring**.*
4) *"You are an **uncomplaining** girl," smiled the doctor.*

Opposite: **impatient**

Pp peaceful

peaceful adjective

Peaceful means quiet and calm.
*Grandma's garden is a **peaceful** place.*

> 1) **quiet** 2) **restful** 3) **serene**

1) *Libraries are **quiet** places.*
2) *Mum felt better after a **restful** sleep.*
3) *The old woman had a **serene** face.*

Opposites: **disturbed, noisy**

perfect adjective

If something is **perfect**, it has no faults.
*Beth did a **perfect** dive.*

> 1) **faultless** 2) **exact** 3) **flawless** 4) **excellent**

1) *The pianist gave a **faultless** performance at the concert.*
2) *Jill drew an **exact** copy of the picture.*
3) *The **flawless** diamond was worth a fortune.*
4) *My new watch keeps **excellent** time.*

Opposites: **imperfect, wrong**

permission noun

If someone gives you **permission**, that person allows you to do something.
*We had **permission** to visit the Forbidden City in Beijing.*

> 1) **consent** 2) **approval** 3) **agreement**

1) *Dad gave his **consent** for us to stay out late.*
2) *We got **approval** of our plans for building a new house.*
3) *"With your **agreement**, I will make a speech," said Mrs Carter.*

Opposite: **refusal**

pet noun

A **pet** is a tame animal you keep in your home.
*I love taking care of my **pets**.*

cat

dog

fish

rabbit

turtle

hamster

pick verb

To **pick** means to choose or select.
*Ellie was asked to **pick** players for her team.*

> 1) **choose** 2) **decide on** 3) **select** 4) **opt for**

1) *Dad always lets Mum **choose** the restaurant.*
2) *Daryl **decided on** the white trainers.*
3) *I want to **select** a new carpet for my bedroom.*
4) *Greg always **opts for** chocolate ice cream.*

Opposite: **reject**

piece noun

A **piece** is a part or a bit of something.
*The waitress gave me a **piece** of apple pie.*

> 1) **bit** 2) **chunk** 3) **scrap** 4) **segment**

1) *The mouse took a **bit** of cheese.*
2) *Daniel handed me a **chunk** of chocolate.*
3) *She picked up a **scrap** of paper from the floor.*
4) *I ate several **segments** of apple during break.*

pile noun

A **pile** is a heap of something.
*There's a **pile** of dirty clothes in the bathroom.*

> 1) **mound** 2) **mountain** 3) **stack**

1) *There is a **mound** of soil in the garden.*
2) *"I have a **mountain** of homework to do," groaned Violet.*
3) *The doctor had a **stack** of mail in the post each morning.*

place noun

A **place** is a particular area.
*My home town is an interesting **place**.*

> 1) **spot** 2) **location** 3) **position**

1) *We found a good **spot** to set up our tent.*
2) *Tony's office moved to a new **location** in the city.*
3) *The hiker marked his exact **position** on the map.*

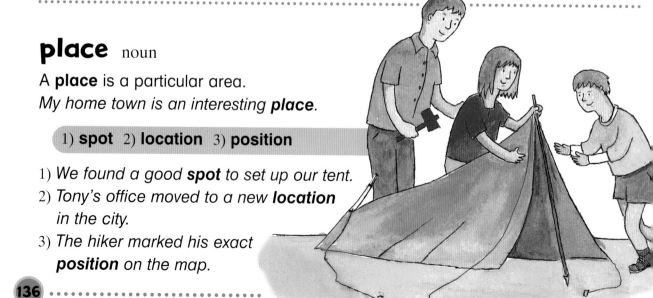

place   verb

To **place** means to put.
*I **placed** my books on the shelf.*

1) **put**   2) **rest**   3) **lay**

1) *"Please **put** your litter in the basket,"*
   said the caretaker.
2) *I **rested** my hands on Clare's shoulders.*
3) *We **lay** fresh flowers on the grave each week.*

planet   noun

We live on a **planet** called Earth.
*These are the nine **planets** in the solar system.*

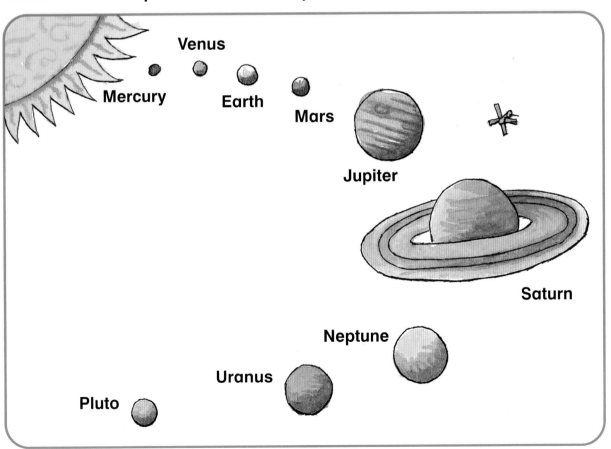

plant noun

A **plant** is a living thing that puts down roots in the soil and grows.
*I bought a flowering **plant** from the nursery.*

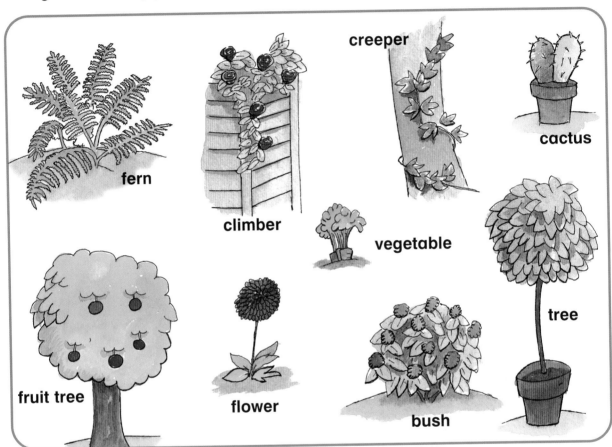

fern

creeper

cactus

climber

vegetable

tree

fruit tree

flower

bush

play verb

To **play** means to amuse yourself or to join in a game.
*Peter liked to **play** on his computer.*

1) **have fun** 2) **frolic** 3) **romp**

1) *The twins love **having fun** with their friends.*
2) *Lambs **frolic** in the fields in spring.*
3) *The boys like to **romp** in the garden.*

Opposite: **work**

please verb

To **please** someone means to make them happy.
*Philip's kindness **pleased** his mother.*

> 1) **satisfy** 2) **gladden** 3) **thrill**

1) *Eve can never **satisfy** her teacher.*
2) *It **gladdens** me to hear birds singing.*
3) *The ballet dancer **thrilled** the audience
   with her performance.*

Opposite: **displease**

poor adjective

To be **poor** means to have little or no money or things.
*The young beggar was very **poor**.*

> 1) **penniless** 2) **destitute** 3) **needy**

1) *She was **penniless** after giving away all her money.*
2) *The **destitute** family had nowhere to live.*
3) *It is kind to give money to **needy** people.*

Opposites: **rich, wealthy**

pretty adjective

To be **pretty** is to be pleasant to look at.
*Jessica wore a **pretty** dress for the dance.*

> 1) **beautiful** 2) **lovely** 3) **gorgeous** 4) **attractive**

1) *Jill had **beautiful** dark-brown hair.*
2) *Grandma bought some **lovely** silk curtains.*
3) *Mr and Mrs Blake lived in a **gorgeous** cottage.*
4) *Jack was an **attractive** boy.*

Opposite: **ugly**

problem noun

A **problem** is a difficulty or question.
*We solved the **problem** of where to hide the treasure.*

1) **trouble** 2) **complication** 3) **worry**

1) *"What's the **trouble**?" asked Mum.*
2) *"Ground Control, we have a **complication**,"*
   said the astronaut.
3) *My main **worry** was that I wouldn't pass my French test.*

proper adjective

Proper means right for the purpose.
*The **proper** place for an oven is in a kitchen.*

1) **correct** 2) **suitable** 3) **fitting**

1) *I put the letters in the **correct** order.*
2) *The library is a **suitable** place to study.*
3) *A shed is not a **fitting** home for a queen.*

Opposites: **improper, wrong**

protect verb

To **protect** means to keep something safe from harm.
*Dad locks his car in the garage to **protect** it from burglars.*

1) **defend** 2) **guard** 3) **shelter** 4) **shield**

1) *The soldiers fired arrows to **defend** the castle.*
2) *Special officers **guard** the king and queen.*
3) *The cat **sheltered** her kittens from the rain.*
4) *I **shielded** my friend from the bullies.*

Opposites: **attack, threaten**

proud adjective

To be **proud** means to be pleased with yourself or someone else for doing well.
*Jim was **proud** of himself for earning a swimming award.*

> 1) **boastful** 2) **pleased** 3) **satisfied**

1) *Mr Green was **boastful** about his clever daughter.*
2) *The students were **pleased** with their test results.*
3) *The pretty girl was **satisfied** with her appearance.*

Opposite: **humble**

pull verb

To **pull** means to drag something or someone towards you.
*The door was stuck, and I had to **pull** hard to open it.*

> 1) **drag** 2) **tow** 3) **haul** 4) **tug**

1) *Beth had to **drag** her heavy bag upstairs.*
2) *Our car **tows** the trailer along the road.*
3) *The teacher **hauled** me out of the pool.*
4) *I had to **tug** at the lead to get my dog to move.*

Opposite: **push**

push verb

To **push** means to force someone or
something away from you.
*The fishermen **push** their boat into the water.*

> 1) **thrust** 2) **press** 3) **shove**

1) *I **thrust** a coin into my brother's hand.*
2) *The man had to **press** on the doorbell.*
3) *Mum **shoved** her way to the front of the line.*

Opposite: **pull**

quarrel verb

To **quarrel** means to argue or disagree angrily.
*Sisters often **quarrel** about borrowing each other's clothes.*

> 1) **argue** 2) **disagree** 3) **fight** 4) **squabble**

1) *Tom and Jack **argue** about whose team is best.*
2) *Mum and Dad **disagree** about what colour to paint the house.*
3) *I don't like **fighting** with my best friend.*
4) *The children **squabble** over their toys.*

Opposite: **agree**

quest noun

A **quest** is an adventure that involves a search.
*The knight's **quest** was to find the dragon.*

> 1) **hunt** 2) **expedition** 3) **mission**

1) *The prince went on a **hunt** for the princess.*
2) *The aim of their **expedition** was to reach the South Pole.*
3) *Billy's **mission** was to find the lost treasure.*

question verb

To **question** means to ask or enquire.
*The teacher **questioned** us about our holidays.*

> 1) **ask** 2) **interrogate** 3) **quiz**

1) *"I want to **ask** you about this broken window,"
   said our neighbour.*
2) *The police officer **interrogated** his suspect.*
3) *We were **quizzed** about the missing bags.*

quick   adjective

If you are **quick**, you are speedy.
*Leroy finished first in the race because he was so **quick**.*

> 1) **swift** 2) **fast** 3) **brisk** 4) **rapid**

1) *Cheetahs are **swift** runners.*
2) *I made a **fast** call before I left the office.*
3) *Dad goes for a **brisk** walk every morning.*
4) *"I am a **rapid** reader," boasted Michelle.*

Opposite: **slow**

quiet   adjective

To be **quiet** means to make little or no sound.
*A mouse is a **quiet** animal.*

> 1) **hushed** 2) **noiseless** 3) **silent** 4) **soundless**

1) *People speak in **hushed** voices in church.*
2) *Charlotte tiptoed on **noiseless** feet.*
3) *"Keep **silent**!" ordered Mr Williams.*
4) *The deer was **soundless** as it ran across the field.*

Opposites: **loud, noisy**

quite   adjective

Quite means completely and utterly.
*The magician was **quite** amazing.*

> 1) **absolutely** 2) **completely** 3) **totally** 4) **fully**

1) *I was **absolutely** sure I had the correct answer.*
2) *"I **completely** agree," said the shop manager.*
3) *Our crossword answers were **totally** wrong.*
4) *The firefighters were **fully** aware of the risks.*

rain noun

Rain is water that falls from the clouds.
*We went out and danced in the **rain**!*

> 1) **shower** 2) **downpour** 3) **drizzle**

1) *The **shower** did not last long.*
2) *"You're not going out in this **downpour**," said Mum.*
3) *I was on my way home when the **drizzle** began.*

raise verb

To **raise** means to lift upwards.
*The nurse had to **raise** Simon's broken leg.*

> 1) **elevate** 2) **escalate** 3) **lift**

1) *If you **elevate** your sprained ankle it will feel better.*
2) *Our local supermarket has **escalated** its prices.*
3) *Beth asked her dad to **lift** her onto his shoulders.*

Opposite: **lower**

ready adjective

If something is **ready**, it is prepared to do something or to be used.
*"Dinner is **ready**!" called Mum.*

> 1) **all set** 2) **primed** 3) **prepared**

1) *We were **all set** to leave until Dad lost the map.*
2) *The class was **primed** for action.*
3) *"Are you **prepared** to face the enemy?" asked the captain.*

Opposites: **unprepared, unready**

real adjective

If something is **real**, it is genuine and not made up.
*Paula's wedding ring had a **real** diamond in it.*

1) **genuine** 2) **true** 3) **honest** 4) **sincere**

1) *The **genuine** princess felt a pea through 100 mattresses.*
2) *My dad is a fireman and a **true** hero.*
3) *"It was an **honest** mistake!" cried Elaine.*
4) *Michael gave his friends a **sincere** apology.*

Opposite: **fake**

refuse verb

To **refuse** means to say "no".
*The boys **refuse** to eat their dinner.*

1) **decline** 2) **deny** 3) **spurn**

1) *Mary **declined** another cup of tea.*
2) *A guard **denied** us entry to the palace.*
3) *The proud girl **spurned** my help.*

Opposite: **accept**

relax verb

To **relax** means to play or take a rest from work.
*I love to **relax** with a good adventure story.*

1) **unwind** 2) **laze** 3) **rest** 4) **calm down**

1) *I **unwind** by playing chess.*
2) *The dog likes to **laze** on my bed.*
3) *Sean tried to **rest** after working in the backyard.*
4) *"I wish you would all **calm down!**" said the teacher.*

remember verb

If you **remember** something, you keep it in your memory.
*George could not **remember** the way to the bookshop.*

> 1) **recall** 2) **recollect** 3) **call to mind**

1) *Grandpa can **recall** the names of his teachers.*
2) *"I don't **recollect** inviting you," said Peter rudely.*
3) *I can't **call to mind** my friend's address.*

Opposite: **forget**

reptile noun

A **reptile** is a cold-blooded animal with a scaly skin.
*All these are different kinds of **reptile**.*

crocodile

snake

turtle

lizard

alligator

tortoise

rescue verb

To **rescue** means to save a person, animal or thing from danger or harm.
*Jim managed to **rescue** the dog from the lake.*

> 1) **free** 2) **salvage** 3) **save**

1) *The man tried to **free** his friend from the trap.*
2) *We could not **salvage** our furniture from the flood.*
3) *The Coast Guard **saves** the lives of many people every year.*

respect verb

To **respect** someone means to look up to them.
*"You should **respect** your elders," said the old man.*

> 1) **admire** 2) **value** 3) **revere**

1) *Lloyd **admires** his father's courage.*
2) *I **value** my friends' opinions.*
3) *The young sailors **revered** their captain.*

Opposite: **disrespect**

rest noun

A **rest** is a period of relaxing or sleeping.
*Kathleen took a **rest** on the bench.*

> 1) **nap** 2) **sleep** 3) **break**

1) *Grandma takes a **nap** every afternoon.*
2) *The short **sleep** did the toddler good.*
3) *"Take a **break**," said the dancing teacher.*

rest *noun*

The **rest** is what is left over.
*The bellboy carried three bags and I took the **rest**.*

> 1) **remainder** 2) **surplus** 3) **balance**

1) *I ate the **remainder** of the chocolate cake.*
2) *The **surplus** had to be thrown away after the party.*
3) *The last ship carried the **balance** of the cargo.*

rich *adjective*

If you are **rich**, you have lots of money or possessions.
*The **rich** man owned a huge Rolls-Royce car.*

> 1) **wealthy** 2) **affluent** 3) **well-to-do**

1) *A **wealthy** family lives in the huge mansion.*
2) *My aunt is an **affluent** woman.*
3) *The **well-to-do** girls wear expensive clothes.*

Opposite: **poor**

right *adjective*

If something is **right**, it is correct.
*I hoped I had the **right** answer.*

> 1) **accurate** 2) **correct** 3) **exact** 3) **precise**

1) *The fortune-teller was **accurate**.*
2) *Jane gave the **correct** answer to the question.*
3) *I gave the customer the **exact** change.*
4) *"What is the **precise** time?" asked Ellie.*

Opposite: **wrong**

risk noun

A **risk** is a chance of loss or danger.
*Jacob took a **risk** when he climbed the high wall.*

> 1) **gamble** 2) **chance** 3) **danger** 4) **hazard**

1) *I took a **gamble** and trusted the burglar.*
2) *There was a **chance** that the tyres might slip on the ice.*
3) *The factory fire was a **danger** to the houses nearby.*
4) *The flood was a **hazard** to people's safety.*

Opposite: **certainty**

rough adjective

If something is **rough**, it is uneven or harsh to the touch.
*A barnacle has a **rough** surface.*

> 1) **bumpy** 2) **craggy** 3) **stony**

1) *He drove the tractor across the **bumpy** field.*
2) *A puffin perched on the **craggy** cliff.*
3) *The plants could not grow in the **stony** ground.*

Opposite: **smooth**

round adjective

Something that is **round** is shaped like a circle.
*We have a **round** mirror over our fireplace.*

> 1) **circular** 2) **curved** 3) **spiral**

1) *The play was performed on a **circular** stage.*
2) *Natalie has graceful, **curved** handwriting.*
3) *There was a beautiful **spiral** staircase
   in the old mansion.*

Rr row

row   noun

A **row** is a line of people or objects.
*There was a **row** of sunflowers in the garden.*

> 1) **chain**   2) **line**   3) **column**

1) *I passed the bucket along the **chain** of people.*
2) *Margaret has a **line** of seashells on her windowsill.*
3) *A **column** of soldiers stood in front of the palace.*

rubbish   noun

Rubbish is something you don't need and throw away.
*We put our **rubbish** in the bin.*

> 1) **litter**   2) **refuse**   3) **waste**   4) **debris**

1) *You should never drop **litter** on the pavement.*
2) *Our **refuse** is collected by a lorry.*
3) *We try to recycle our **waste**.*
4) *The **debris** was put in rubbish bags.*

rude   adjective

If you are **rude**, you are impolite.
*The **rude** girl stuck out her tongue at her friend.*

> 1) **bad-mannered**   2) **curt**   3) **surly**   4) **insulting**

1) *The **bad-mannered** boy shouted at his mum.*
2) *"Shut up!" said Robin in a **curt** voice.*
3) *I did not like the reporter's **surly** tone.*
4) *The sergeant spoke in an **insulting** way.*

Opposite: **polite**

ruin verb

To **ruin** something means to damage it so it can't be fixed.
*The mud on Mickey's boots **ruined** the new carpet.*

> 1) **wreck** 2) **demolish** 3) **destroy** 4) **spoil**

1) *Cindy wanted to **wreck** my stamp collection.*
2) *The waves **demolished** our sandcastle.*
3) *The ugly building **destroyed** the beautiful view.*
4) *Sebastian **spoiled** his painting by spilling water on it.*

rule noun

A **rule** is an instruction that tells you what you may or may not do.
*We learned the **rules** before we played the game.*

> 1) **law** 2) **regulation** 3) **decree**

1) *The police make sure that people obey the **law**.*
2) *There are strict **regulations** against cruelty to animals.*
3) *In 'Sleeping Beauty' the king makes a **decree** that there are to be no spinning wheels in his kingdom.*

rule verb

To **rule** something means to be in charge of it.
*"I **rule** this kingdom," shouted the bad-tempered king.*

> 1) **control** 2) **govern** 3) **lead** 4) **run**

1) *The pilot **controls** the aeroplane.*
2) *The new chief **governs** the children's hospital.*
3) *A young woman **leads** the reading group.*
4) *The brothers **run** a little coffee shop.*

rumour noun

A **rumour** is a story passed from one person to another, which may not be true.
*We heard a **rumour** that our history teacher is leaving.*

> 1) **gossip** 2) **talk** 3) **hearsay**

1) *There is a lot of **gossip** about our next-door neighbours.*
2) *"Have you heard all the **talk** about the mayor going to prison?" asked Dad.*
3) *"That story is only **hearsay**," said the TV announcer.*

run verb

To **run** means to move quickly.
*Dad had to **run** to catch the bus.*

> 1) **sprint** 2) **dart** 3) **dash** 4) **scamper**

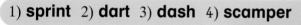

1) *I can **sprint** faster than all my friends.*
2) *Ben had to **dart** undercover when it started to rain.*
3) *He **dashed** to the store before it closed.*
4) *The kittens **scampered** around the room.*

rush verb

To **rush** means to hurry.
*We had to **rush** to get there on time.*

> 1) **hurry** 2) **fly** 3) **scramble**

1) *Everyone **hurried** home after school.*
2) *"I must **fly**!" panted Mrs Harris when it started to rain.*
3) *We **scrambled** to be first in line for tickets.*

Opposite: **dawdle**

sad adjective

To be **sad** means to be unhappy.
*Jill was **sad** that she had broken her favourite soft toy.*

> 1) **unhappy** 2) **miserable** 3) **blue**

1) *Dad was **unhappy** because his car had broken down.*
2) *The girl was **miserable** because her holiday was over.*
3) *Conrad felt **blue** when his dog went missing.*

Opposites: **cheerful, glad, happy**

safe adjective

If something is **safe**, it is free from danger or harm.
*It is **safe** to skate on the ice.*

> 1) **secure** 2) **protected** 3) **unharmed**

1) *I felt **secure** when all the doors were locked.*
2) *The princess was always **protected** from danger.*
3) *"Make sure the animals are **unharmed**," said the zookeeper.*

Opposites: **dangerous, unsafe**

same adjective

Things that are the **same** are exactly like each other.
*Mary and Jenny wore the **same** dresses.*

> 1) **alike** 2) **identical** 3) **matching**

1) *My mum and her older sister look **alike**.*
2) *My brother and I are **identical** twins.*
3) *The ski team wore **matching** sweaters.*

Opposite: **different**

save verb

To **save** means to store something for use in the future.
Megan wanted to save her money.

> 1) **keep** 2) **hoard** 3) **hold on to**

1) *I keep all my old ticket stubs.*
2) *Misers like to hoard their money.*
3) *Tom held on to his allowance so he could buy his mum a present.*

Opposites: **spend, waste**

say verb

To **say** means to speak words.
Jean would not say where she had been.

> 1) **utter** 2) **state** 3) **remark** 4) **exclaim**

1) *The stranger did not utter a word.*
2) *"Please state your name," said the judge.*
3) *The babysitter remarked that it was bedtime.*
4) *"Leave me alone!" I exclaimed.*

scare verb

To **scare** means to frighten.
Billy put on a vampire mask to scare me.

> 1) **alarm** 2) **terrify** 3) **startle**

1) *"Don't alarm Grandma by shouting," warned Dad.*
2) *Fireworks terrify my pet cat.*
3) *I was startled by the loud bang.*

scream verb

To **scream** means to yell loudly.
*Annette **screamed** when she saw the ghost.*

1) **yell** 2) **screech** 3) **shriek**

1) *I **yelled** as the car rolled backwards.*
2) *"Don't **screech** in my ear!" complained Mum.*
3) *The sick baby **shrieked** for hours.*

seat noun

A **seat** is something made to sit on.
*My favourite **seat** is soft and cosy.*

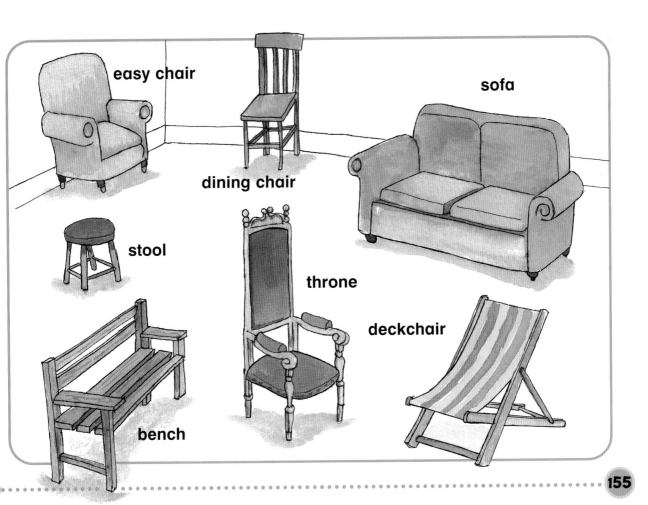

easy chair

dining chair

sofa

stool

throne

deckchair

bench

secret   adjective

If something is **secret**, it is not to be told
or shown to others.
*We have a **secret** club.*

  1) **private** 2) **concealed** 3) **hidden** 4) **unknown**

1) *I write my **private** thoughts in my diary.*
2) *"I'll put your jewels in the **concealed** safe,"
   said the manager.*
3) *The desk has a **hidden** compartment.*
4) *Collette's **unknown** admirer sent her red roses.*

see   verb

To **see** means to observe with your eyes.
*I can **see** the mountains from my bedroom window.*

  1) **glimpse** 2) **spot** 3) **witness**

1) *Rosina did not **glimpse** any fairies.*
2) *"Did you **spot** the butterfly?"
   asked Mum eagerly.*
3) *I **witnessed** the rail accident.*

selfish   adjective

To be **selfish** means to think only about your own needs and wishes.
*It was **selfish** of Owen to drink all the water.*

  1) **greedy** 2) **self-centred** 3) **ungenerous**

1) *The **greedy** woman left no food for the children.*
2) *We taught our **self-centred** friend a lesson.*
3) *An **ungenerous** person had taken the last blanket.*

Opposite: **generous**

send verb

To **send** something means to direct it to another place.
Daisy had to send a letter to her friend Sarah.

> 1) **mail** 2) **dispatch** 3) **forward** 4) **transmit**

1) *I **mail** a letter to my aunt once a week.*
2) *People **dispatch** thousands of packages every day.*
3) *My boss asked me to **forward** his mail to him.*
4) *Diana **transmits** emails to all her friends.*

Opposite: **receive**

sensible adjective

If something is **sensible**, it is wise.
*It is **sensible** to wear warm clothes in the winter.*

> 1) **wise** 2) **practical** 3) **reasonable**

1) *The professor always gives **wise** advice.*
2) *The builder had some **practical** ideas.*
3) *It was **reasonable** to ask for a lunch break.*

Opposites: **silly, unwise**

serious adjective

If something is **serious**, it is important or worrying.
*Everyone looks very **serious** in the old photo.*

> 1) **grave** 2) **solemn** 3) **long-faced**

1) *Dad looked **grave** when he told us the bad news.*
2) *We were very **solemn** when we met the judge.*
3) *The **long-faced** man did not laugh at the joke.*

Opposite: **light-hearted**

shake verb

To **shake** means to move quickly up and down or back and forth.
*The heavy dinosaur made the ground **shake** when it moved.*

1) **quiver** 2) **shiver** 3) **shudder** 4) **tremble**

1) *I saw the leaves **quiver** in the breeze.*
2) *Most people **shiver** if they are cold.*
3) *Scary stories can make you **shudder**.*
4) *The little dog **trembled** with fear.*

shape noun

The **shape** of something is the form you make if you draw a line around its outside edges.
*An orange has a round **shape**.*

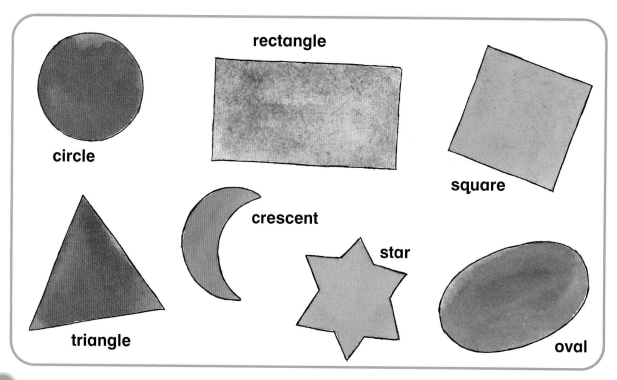

rectangle

circle

square

crescent

star

triangle

oval

share verb

To **share** means to divide something between a number of people.
*We **shared** our food on the camping trip.*

> 1) **divide** 2) **split** 3) **distribute**

1) *Dad **divided** the prize money between us.*
2) *I **split** the cake into four equal pieces.*
3) *The jobs were **distributed** among the three men.*

sharp adjective

If something is **sharp**, it is pointed and could cut you.
*The **sharp** scissors cut through the paper.*

> 1) **pointed** 2) **keen** 3) **cutting**

1) *The seamstress pricked her finger on the **pointed** needle.*
2) *The pirate captain's sword had a **keen** blade.*
3) *"The **cutting** edge of a knife is dangerous,"
said the cook.*

Opposite: **blunt**

shine verb

If something **shines**, it glows brightly.
*My silver ring **shines** in the sun.*

> 1) **beam** 2) **gleam** 3) **glitter** 4) **sparkle**

1) *The moonlight **beams** through my curtains.*
2) *A light was **gleaming** in the library window.*
3) *The little girl's eyes **glittered** with excitement.*
4) *The sunlight **sparkled** on the water.*

shoe noun

A **shoe** is a covering you wear on your foot.
*"Put your **shoes** on before you go out," said Dad.*

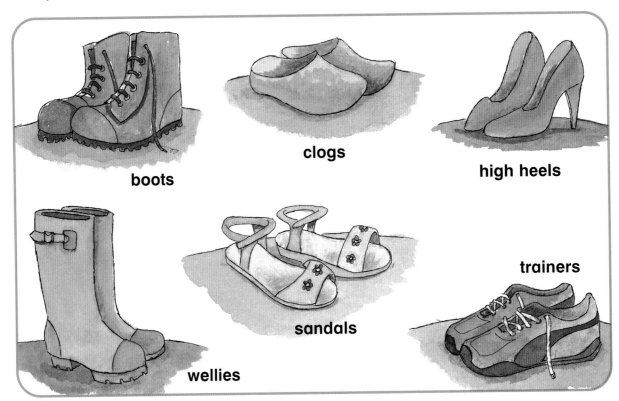

clogs

boots

high heels

trainers

sandals

wellies

short adjective

Something **short** is less than usual height or length.
*The carpenter picked up a **short** plank of wood.*

1) **little** 2) **small** 3) **squat**

1) *I bought a **little** tree to plant in my garden.*
2) *"You are too **small** to go on that ride,"
   the man told Jamie.*
3) *Our neighbour is a **squat** woman.*

Opposites: **long**, **tall**

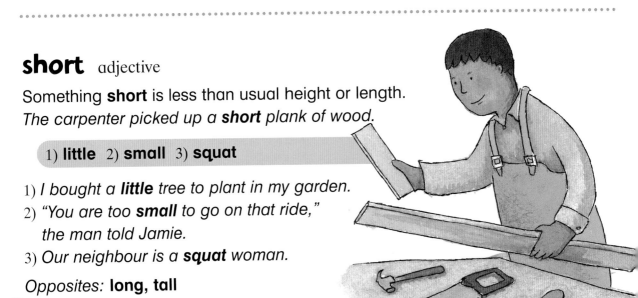

shout verb

To **shout** means to call out loudly.
*Ben had to **shout** to make his friend hear.*

1) **bellow** 2) **yell** 3) **bawl** 4) **roar**

1) *The coach had to **bellow** at the players.*
2) *Dad began to **yell** when his team scored.*
3) *I **bawled** at my friend across the playground.*
4) *"Don't do that!" **roared** the teacher.*

Opposite: **whisper**

show verb

To **show** means to allow something to be seen.
*The soldiers were proud to **show** their medals to us.*

1) **reveal** 2) **display** 3) **present**

1) *I pulled off my mask to **reveal** my face.*
2) *Maggie **displays** her sculptures in the art gallery.*
3) *The lawyer **presents** her evidence to the jury.*

Opposite: **hide**

shy adjective

A **shy** person is nervous with strangers.
*My **shy** cousin blushed when I spoke to her.*

1) **timid** 2) **bashful** 3) **meek**

1) *The **timid** dog put his tail between his legs.*
2) *Lewis was **bashful** around girls.*
3) *The new recruit spoke in a **meek** voice.*

Opposite: **outgoing**

silent   adjective

To be **silent** means to make no noise.
*The manager was **silent** while she listened
to our complaint.*

> 1) **quiet**   2) **noiseless**   3) **soundless**

1) *"Be **quiet**!" snapped the librarian.*
2) *The burglars were **noiseless** when they
broke into the house.*
3) *Roland danced on **soundless** feet.*

Opposite: **noisy**

silly   adjective

If something is **silly**, it is not sensible.
*Dad told us to stop being **silly**.*

> 1) **absurd**   2) **foolish**   3) **idiotic**   4) **unwise**

1) *"That's an **absurd** idea!" laughed Sonia.*
2) *The clowns played **foolish** games.*
3) *Our **idiotic** dog loves chasing his own tail.*
4) *It is **unwise** to trust a liar.*

Opposites: **sensible, wise**

simple   adjective

If something is **simple**, it is easy to do or understand.
*Beth liked doing **simple** maths problems.*

> 1) **easy**   2) **clear**   3) **plain**

1) *Our chemistry teacher showed us an **easy** way to do the experiment.*
2) *"The answer is **clear**," said the teacher.*
3) *It was **plain** to see who was in charge.*

Opposites: **complicated, difficult**

sleep verb

When you **sleep**, you close your eyes and rest.
*I can't **sleep** with the light on.*

1) **nap** 2) **snooze** 3) **doze** 4) **slumber**

1) *Grandpa likes to **nap** in the sun.*
2) *Cats **snooze** whenever they can.*
3) *The baby **dozed** in his cot.*
4) *Dad **slumbered** while we watched a film.*

Opposite: **awaken**

slide verb

To **slide** means to move slowly along a surface.
*It is fun to **slide** on the ice.*

1) **glide** 2) **skate** 3) **slip** 4) **skid**

1) *The dancers **glide** across the floor.*
2) *I love to **skate** at the ice rink.*
3) *"Dad **slipped** on a banana skin," giggled Suzy.*
4) *We **skid** on the kitchen floor when it has been polished.*

slow adjective

If something is **slow**, it takes a long time.
*Tortoises are **slow** walkers.*

1) **lazy** 2) **plodding** 3) **leisurely**

1) *Mrs Hawkins is a **lazy** worker.*
2) *The man walked with **plodding** steps.*
3) *We took a **leisurely** stroll to the shop.*

Opposites: **fast, quick**

small adjective

If something is **small**, it is little or tiny.
*The **small** boy could not reach the book on the shelf.*

> 1) **little** 2) **miniature** 3) **tiny**

1) *The baby wore **little** mittens.*
2) *I bought a **miniature** table for my doll's house.*
3) *A bumblebee has **tiny** wings.*

Opposites: **big, huge, large**

smell noun

A **smell** is something that your nose detects.
*I held my nose to keep out the fishy **smell**.*

> 1) **odour** 2) **scent** 3) **fragrance** 4) **aroma**

1) *The sweaty trainers had a horrible **odour**.*
2) *Dogs can track people by following their **scent**.*
3) *Flowers give off a lovely **fragrance**.*
4) *"What a wonderful **aroma**!" cried the hungry man.*

smooth adjective

If something is **smooth**, it has no bumps or roughness.
*A squash ball has a **smooth** surface.*

> 1) **glossy** 2) **polished** 3) **shiny** 4) **sleek**

1) *I wrote my invitations on **glossy** paper.*
2) *Dad gave the table a **polished** finish.*
3) *My sister has lovely, **shiny** hair.*
4) *I like to stroke my cat's **sleek** coat.*

Opposites: **coarse, rough**

soft adjective

If something is **soft**, it is easy to dent it or change its shape.
*We made biscuits with the **soft** dough.*

> 1) **spongy** 2) **cushioned** 3) **flexible**

1) *I bounced on the **spongy** mattress.*
2) *Anthony sank into the **cushioned** easy chair.*
3) *The man heated the glass until it was **flexible**.*

Opposite: **hard**

sorry adjective

If you are **sorry**, you feel bad about something you
have said or done.
*"I'm **sorry** I broke the vase," said Kitty.*

> 1) **apologetic** 2) **ashamed** 3) **regretful** 4) **remorseful**

1) *The waiter was **apologetic** about the horrible food.*
2) *We felt **ashamed** that we had not believed our friend.*
3) *I am **regretful** that I lost my temper.*
4) *The **remorseful** bully asked us to forgive him.*

Opposite: **remorseless**

sort noun

A **sort** is a brand, a group, or a kind.
*"What **sort** of cake should we buy?" I asked.*

> 1) **type** 2) **kind** 3) **brand**

1) *Colin likes all **types** of music.*
2) *We saw many **kinds** of bird on our walk.*
3) *I always use the same **brand** of toothpaste.*

Ss spare

spare adjective

If something is **spare**, it is extra or more than is needed.
*There was a **spare** seat next to me in the theatre.*

> 1) **additional** 2) **extra** 3) **leftover**

1) *We had five **additional** tickets.*
2) *"Who would like the **extra** mushrooms?" asked Dad.*
3) *There were six **leftover** glasses.*

speak verb

To **speak** means to talk.
*Matilda's best friend would not **speak** to her.*

> 1) **talk** 2) **chat** 3) **converse**

1) *You should not **talk** in assembly.*
2) *I **chat** to my friends on the phone for hours.*
3) *Joseph enjoys **conversing** with his grandpa.*

special adjective

If something is **special**, it is important and unusual.
*Eliza won a very **special** prize in the competition.*

> 1) **significant** 2) **important** 3) **unique**

1) *Your birthday is a **significant** day.*
2) *"You are very **important** to me," Hugh said.*
3) *The ancient vase was a **unique** design.*

Opposites: **common, ordinary**

speed verb

To **speed** means to move very quickly.
*I always **speed** home from school.*

> 1) **race** 2) **hurry** 3) **rush** 4) **zoom**

1) *Polly had to **race** to be on time.*
2) *"**Hurry** up and get changed,"
   said the sports teacher.*
3) *The fans **rushed** to see the film star.*
4) *We **zoomed** down the road on our roller skates.*

Opposite: **crawl**

spin verb

To **spin** means to turn around very quickly.
*When I **spin** around I get dizzy.*

> 1) **twirl** 2) **whirl** 3) **revolve**

1) *Jasmine **twirled** to show off her new dress.*
2) *The fallen leaves **whirled** in the strong wind.*
3) *The hotel doors **revolve** to let people in and out.*

spoil verb

To **spoil** something means to ruin it.
*The wind **spoiled** Jessica's hairdo.*

> 1) **ruin** 2) **damage** 3) **wreck** 4) **destroy**

1) *Grass stains **ruined** my new dress.*
2) *Too much water can **damage** plants.*
3) *A terrible storm **wrecked** our garden.*
4) *"I'm going to **destroy** your artwork," snarled the protester.*

sport noun

A **sport** is a game you play to win or to have fun.
*My brother plays **sport** at school on Mondays.*

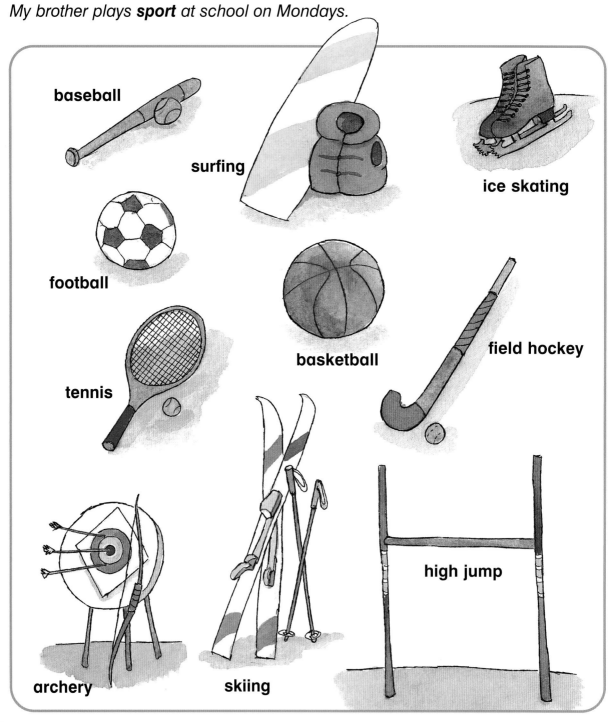

baseball

surfing

ice skating

football

basketball

field hockey

tennis

archery

skiing

high jump

start verb

To **start** something is to begin it or make it begin.
*At the **start** of the race Jack was in the lead.*

> 1) **begin** 2) **open** 3) **set up**

1) *"**Begin** on page five," said the teacher.*
2) *She **opened** the game by throwing out the first ball.*
3) *My cousin **set up** the school drama club.*

Opposites: **end, finish**

stay verb

To **stay** means to remain.
*Fred had to **stay** inside because he had a cold.*

> 1) **remain** 2) **settle** 3) **linger**

1) *It started to rain so we **remained** in the car.*
2) *The family decided to **settle** in Canada.*
3) *My sister wants to **linger** with me.*

Opposites: **go, leave**

stop verb

To **stop** something means to end it.
*Dad could not **stop** us from arguing.*

> 1) **cease** 2) **finish** 3) **halt**

1) *The noise **ceased** at midnight.*
2) *I **finish** work at five every day.*
3) *The police officer tried to **halt** the traffic.*

Opposite: **start**

story noun

A **story** is a description of real or made-up events.
*Patrick did not believe his friend's **story**.*

> 1) **tale** 2) **account** 3) **fairy tale** 4) **legend**

1) *The class listened to the exciting **tale**.*
2) *I gave my **account** of what had happened.*
3) *"Read me a **fairy tale**," begged the little girl.*
4) *We like to hear about the **legend** of Robin Hood.*

strange adjective

If something is **strange**, it is odd or unusual.
*There was a **strange** smell coming from the oven.*

> 1) **curious** 2) **weird** 3) **odd** 4) **peculiar**

1) *Grandpa told us a **curious** story.*
2) *"Can you hear that **weird** noise?" asked Harriet.*
3) *The man had an **odd** way of walking.*
4) *John got a **peculiar** letter in the post.*

Opposites: **common, ordinary, usual**

strict adjective

To be **strict** means to be severe about obeying the rules.
*Our teacher is **strict** but fair.*

> 1) **firm** 2) **severe** 3) **stern** 4) **harsh**

1) *The library has **firm** rules about how many books you can borrow.*
2) *The old lady's **severe** expression scared George.*
3) *The **stern** coach would not let anyone talk during football practice.*
4) *Mandy was upset by her brother's **harsh** words.*

strong adjective

To be **strong** means to have great power or force.
*Uncle Ernie is a **strong** man.*

1) **tough** 2) **stout** 3) **sturdy**

1) *"I'm as **tough** as iron!" grinned Dad.*
2) *A swing dangled from the **stout** tree in our garden.*
3) *The **sturdy** boy carried his bike across the stream.*

Opposite: **weak**

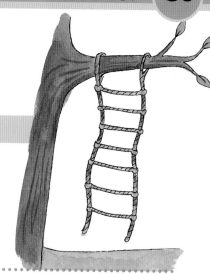

stupid adjective

To be **stupid** means to be unintelligent.
*The **stupid** boy put his head in a lion's mouth.*

1) **brainless** 2) **dense** 3) **dim** 4) **foolish**

1) *Our **brainless** dog thinks he's a pig.*
2) *Dylan is **dense** when it comes to history.*
3) *The cat is **dim** but we love him.*
4) *Crossing a road from between parked cars is a **foolish** thing to do.*

Opposites: **clever, intelligent, smart**

sudden adjective

If something is **sudden**, it is fast or not expected.
*My **sudden** movement scared the feeding birds.*

1) **abrupt** 2) **surprising** 3) **quick** 4) **unexpected**

1) *The ballet came to an **abrupt** end when the stage collapsed.*
2) *The mystery story had a **surprising** twist at the end.*
3) *The car took a **quick** right turn.*
4) *An **unexpected** visitor arrived at the house.*

Opposite: **gradual**

sulk verb

To **sulk** is to be quiet because you are angry or in a bad mood.
*You shouldn't **sulk** just because you didn't win the game.*

> 1) **brood** 2) **mope** 3) **scowl**

1) *Anna couldn't stop **brooding** about her silly mistake.*
2) *My brother just **mopes** around the house all day.*
3) *Sarah **scowled** when Dad didn't give her any sweets.*

sure adjective

If something is **sure**, it is not in doubt.
*The racehorse was a **sure** winner.*

> 1) **certain** 2) **positive** 3) **definite**

1) *The farmer was **certain** that his bull had won first prize.*
2) *The old woman was **positive** she had seen the doctor before.*
3) *Fred had a **definite** reason for wanting to go on the school trip.*

surprise noun

A **surprise** is something you did not expect.
*My birthday party was a big **surprise**.*

> 1) **shock** 2) **blow** 3) **bombshell** 4) **jolt**

1) *It was a **shock** to see all the storm damage.*
2) *Failing the French test was a **blow** for Meg.*
3) *Emma's news about her move was a **bombshell**.*
4) *The film's unexpected ending gave the audience a **jolt**.*

HAPPY BIRTHDAY

take verb

To **take** means to get hold of something.
*The bullies **take** Bobby's lunch money.*

> 1) **seize** 2) **grasp** 3) **clutch**

1) *I **seized** the oars and rowed away.*
2) *"Try to **grasp** the rope!" shouted the climber.*
3) *The nervous girl **clutched** her father's hand.*

Opposite: **give**

talk verb

To **talk** means to say words.
*We were told not to **talk** in class.*

> 1) **chat** 2) **speak** 3) **tell**

1) *We **chatted** all the way home.*
2) *"Don't **speak** to anyone you don't know," said my dad.*
3) *My best friend came over to **tell** me about the party.*

No talking in class!

tall adjective

To be **tall** means to be above normal height.
*Peter was **tall** for his age.*

> 1) **big** 2) **high** 3) **lanky** 4) **towering**

1) *The **big** boys played on the football team.*
2) *The **high** wall was hard to climb.*
3) *Leo was a **lanky** teenager.*
4) *The **towering** building seemed to touch the clouds.*

Opposites: **low, short, small**

teacher noun

A **teacher** is someone whose job is helping others to learn.
*Miss Brooks is our new **teacher**.*

> 1) **instructor** 2) **tutor** 3) **professor**

1) *I was scared of skiing, but my **instructor** helped me.*
2) *Kara had a private **tutor** to teach her advanced maths.*
3) *"Pay attention in class!" shouted the **professor**.*

tear verb

To **tear** means to rip.
*I didn't mean to **tear** my new trousers.*

> 1) **rip** 2) **slit** 3) **split**

1) *Nicholas **ripped** his father's travel diary.*
2) *The thorns **slit** holes in my jacket.*
3) *"You've **split** your top," said the dressmaker.*

tell verb

To **tell** means to give information in words.
*Annie and Amy like to **tell** each other secrets.*

> 1) **announce** 2) **confess** 3) **state** 4) **notify**

1) *Matthew and Emma wanted to **announce**
   their engagement.*
2) *The accused decided to **confess** the truth.*
3) *The witness had to **state** how the accident happened.*
4) *"Please **notify** me when you feel better," said the doctor.*

temper noun

A **temper** is an angry mood.
*Lisa frowns when she is in a **temper**.*

1) **rage** 2) **tantrum** 3) **fury**

1) *Our teacher was in a **rage** because we were late.*
2) *My naughty little brother threw a **tantrum**.*
3) *My mum flew into a **fury** when she saw my bedroom.*

thankful adjective

If you are **thankful**, you are grateful.
*Beth was **thankful** that Aunt Aggie remembered her birthday.*

1) **appreciative** 2) **grateful** 3) **relieved**

1) *Mum was **appreciative** of our help when we went camping.*
2) *Grandma was **grateful** to get the box of plums.*
3) *"We're **relieved** that we've passed our exams," said the students.*

Opposites: **thankless, unappreciative, ungrateful**

thick adjective

To be **thick** means to be large in width or depth.
*The room was covered in a **thick** layer of dust.*

1) **broad** 2) **wide** 3) **deep**

1) *The wrestler puffed out his **broad** chest.*
2) *My sister drew a **wide** line across our bedroom floor.*
3) *We walked through the **deep** blanket of snow.*

Opposite: **thin**

thin adjective

To be **thin** means to be small in width or depth.
*My cousin Alice is tall and very **thin**.*

> 1) **skinny** 2) **slender** 3) **lean** 4) **slim**

1) *"You are too **skinny**," said Dr Hurst.*
2) *A breeze shook the **slender** tree.*
3) *The stray dog was scruffy and **lean**.*
4) *Brian gave his girlfriend a **slim** book of poetry.*

Opposites: **fat, thick**

thing noun

Thing is a word to describe any object that is not alive.
*"What is that **thing**?" asked Lara.*

> 1) **article** 2) **object** 3) **item**

1) *The fishermen threw some **articles** into the sea.*
2) *I did not know what the stone **objects** in the museum were.*
3) *The strange **items** glowed in the dark.*

think verb

To **think** means to form ideas in your mind.
*John tried hard to **think** of an answer.*

> 1) **ponder** 2) **consider** 3) **reason** 4) **muse**

1) *The poet sat down to **ponder**.*
2) *I did not **consider** that I was wrong.*
3) *The hikers **reasoned** they should go south.*
4) *"There can only be one answer,"*
   ***mused** the detective.*

throw verb

To **throw** means to send something through the air using
your arm and hand.
*The new bowler can **throw** a ball a long way.*

1) **fling** 2) **hurl** 3) **toss** 4) **pitch**

1) *I was told to **fling** the confetti at the bride.*
2) *"Don't **hurl** crayons across the room!"
   said Miss Frost.*
3) *The baby **tossed** her rattle out of the buggy.*
4) *The captain **pitched** a fast ball.*

Opposite: **catch**

thud noun

A **thud** is the sound of something heavy hitting a surface.
*The rider hit the ground with a **thud**.*

1) **bang** 2) **clunk** 3) **thump**

1) *There was a loud **bang** when the worker
   dropped his hammer.*
2) *A noisy **clunk** made everyone jump.*
3) *Jill fell to the floor with a **thump**.*

tidy adjective

Tidy means neat and in order.
*My brother has a **tidy** bedroom.*

1) **neat** 2) **orderly** 3) **well-kept**

1) *Alana's clothes are **neat** and clean.*
2) *Mr Lee has an **orderly** classroom.*
3) *Lots of visitors came to see the
   well-kept gardens.*

Opposites: **messy, untidy**

tight adjective

If something is **tight**, it fits with no room to spare.
*The young skier wore a **tight** jacket.*

> 1) **close-fitting** 2) **cramped** 3) **snug**

1) *I chose a **close-fitting** sweater.*
2) *Space was **cramped** in the crowded train.*
3) *Gail's shoes were a bit too **snug**.*

Opposite: **loose**

tiny adjective

If something is **tiny**, it is very small.
*I saw a **tiny** mouse on top of the cupboard.*

> 1) **little** 2) **minute** 3) **small**

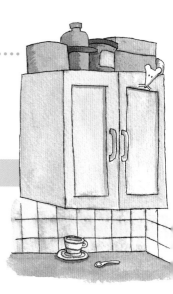

1) *The children love their **little** rabbit.*
2) *Hazel was scared of the **minute** spider.*
3) *The woodsman had a **small** cut on his hand.*

Opposites: **big, huge, large**

tired adjective

If you are **tired**, you feel that you need
to rest.
*The soldiers were too **tired** to keep marching.*

> 1) **exhausted** 2) **weary** 3) **worn out** 4) **sleepy**

1) *The **exhausted** children went to sleep early.*
2) *"You look **weary**," said Mum.*
3) *I was **worn out** from running the race.*
4) *We were too **sleepy** to watch the late film.*

Opposites: **energetic, fresh**

tool noun

A **tool** is an instrument you use to help you do a job.
A rake is a gardening tool.

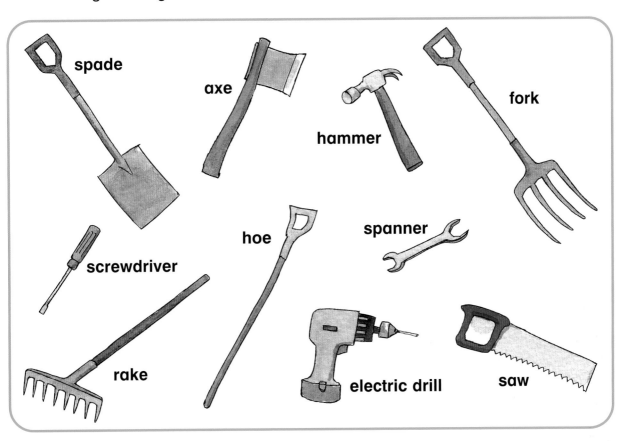

spade

axe

hammer

fork

hoe

spanner

screwdriver

rake

electric drill

saw

top noun

The **top** is the highest part.
Freddy climbed to the top of the mountain.

1) **tip** 2) **crown** 3) **peak**

1) *The tip of the iceberg poked out of the sea.*
2) *Dad is going bald at the crown of his head.*
3) *The climber reached the mountain's peak.*

Opposites: **base, bottom**

topic noun

A **topic** is a subject.
*"Today's **topic** is underwater life," said Mr Wells.*

> 1) **subject** 2) **theme** 3) **issue**

1) *The students had a choice of three **subjects**.*
2) *Magic was the **theme** of Lauren's story.*
3) *Everyone at the meeting wanted to discuss a different **issue**.*

total adjective

If something is **total**, it is complete.
*Our school play was a **total** success.*

> 1) **complete** 2) **absolute** 3) **utter**

1) *"You are a **complete** idiot,"
   said Nicole.*
2) *The game was an **absolute** bore.*
3) *My grandpa is an **utter** genius.*

Opposite: **partial**

total noun

The **total** is the sum of several amounts added together.
*I counted the money and worked out the **total**.*

> 1) **amount** 2) **entirety** 3) **sum**

1) *The **amount** was enough to buy a car.*
2) *We emptied our piggy banks and
   gave the **entirety** to charity.*
3) *I added the numbers and showed
   the **sum** to my teacher.*

touch verb

To **touch** something means to feel it.
*Mark had to **touch** the button to make the lamp work.*

> 1) **handle** 2) **feel** 3) **pat**

1) *When I **handled** the vase I broke it.*
2) *Courtney reached out to **feel** the dress.*
3) *Mum said I could **pat** the dog.*

tough adjective

To be **tough** means to be strong and sturdy.
*Soldiers have to be brave and **tough**.*

> 1) **hardy** 2) **brawny** 3) **sturdy**

1) *The **hardy** tents kept out the rain.*
2) *"I need a **brawny** helper to carry this box," said Miss Robson.*
3) *There is a **sturdy** table in our playroom.*

Opposite: **weak**

trap verb

To **trap** something means to catch or hold it so
that it cannot escape.
*The cruel boy **trapped** a wasp under a glass.*

> 1) **capture** 2) **catch** 3) **corner**

1) *The rangers tried to **capture** the lion.*
2) *We tried to **catch** the runaway mouse.*
3) *The officers **cornered** the robbers.*

Opposite: **release**

travel verb

To **travel** means to go from one place to another.
*I have to **travel** for two hours to see my uncle.*

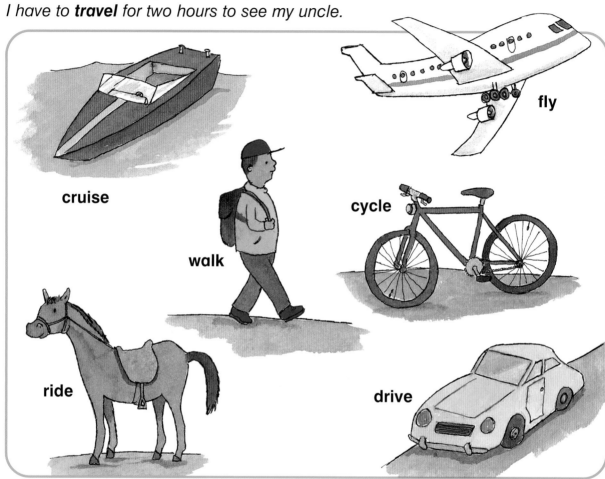

cruise

fly

walk

cycle

ride

drive

treasure noun

Treasure is something of great value or worth.
*The pirates' **treasure** was gold and jewels.*

1) **wealth** 2) **fortune** 3) **riches**

1) *"I will give away my **wealth**,"*
   said the generous woman.
2) *The gambler lost his family **fortune**.*
3) *The millionaire hid his **riches** in a safe.*

treat verb

How you **treat** someone is how you behave towards that person.
*Kyle's foster parents **treat** him well.*

> 1) **deal with** 2) **handle** 3) **use**

1) *"I **deal with** every player fairly," said the umpire.*
2) *Dr Morgan **handles** her patients with kindness.*
3) *"**Use** the lab equipment carefully," said our teacher.*

trick verb

To **trick** someone is to fool them or play a joke on them.
*Rob **tricked** his mum into answering the doorbell.*

> 1) **fool** 2) **deceive** 3) **cheat**

1) *Jennifer **fooled** me into thinking I had won a big prize.*
2) *A dishonest salesperson **deceived** her by selling a fake diamond ring.*
3) *He won the card game by **cheating** when no one was looking.*

true adjective

If something is **true**, it is real or factual.
*Everything the reporter said was **true**.*

> 1) **correct** 2) **genuine** 3) **real**

1) *Only I knew the **correct** answer.*
2) *Wesley has a **genuine** love of snakes.*
3) *The spy told no one his **real** name.*

Opposites: **false, untrue**

trust verb

To **trust** someone means to have confidence in them.
*I **trust** all my friends to tell me the truth.*

> 1) **believe** 2) **count on** 3) **depend on**

1) *The store manager **believed** the customer when no one else did.*
2) *"Can I **count on** you to keep a secret?" asked Chloe.*
3) *You can never **depend on** my sister to be on time.*

Opposite: **mistrust**

try verb

To **try** something means to make an effort
to do it.
*Jacob wants to **try** to learn to dive.*

> 1) **aim** 2) **attempt** 3) **strive**

1) *Our team captain always **aims** to win.*
2) *The climbers will **attempt** to climb the
   highest peak in the mountain range.*
3) *Good competitors always **strive** to do their best.*

turn verb

To **turn** means to move in a circular direction.
*The wheels **turn** to make the car move.*

> 1) **revolve** 2) **rotate** 3) **spin** 4) **pivot**

1) *The model **revolved** to face the artist.*
2) *The planets **rotate** around the sun.*
3) *Some performers can **spin** plates on sticks.*
4) *A basketball player **pivots** on the spot.*

ugly adjective

If something is **ugly**, it is not nice to look at.
*Everyone was scared of the **ugly** witch.*

> 1) **homely** 2) **hideous** 3) **unattractive**

1) *"You are a **homely** girl," said the woman rudely.*
2) *The monster had a **hideous** face.*
3) *Laura wore an **unattractive** coat.*

Opposites: **beautiful, pretty**

uncover verb

To **uncover** something means to take the cover off it or show it to others.
*The chef **uncovered** the pan.*

> 1) **expose** 2) **reveal** 3) **unmask**

1) *I pulled off the cloth to **expose** the table.*
2) *The detective wanted to **reveal** the truth.*
3) *The security guard **unmasked** the real thief.*

Opposites: **conceal, cover, hide**

under preposition

If something is **under**, it is below.
*The farmer put the newborn lamb **under** his coat to keep it warm.*

> 1) **below** 2) **beneath** 3) **underneath**

1) *Alfred put the basket **below** the stairs.*
2) *The old woman hid the dog **beneath** her chair.*
3) *"Put the box **underneath** the table," said Miss Fox.*

understand verb

To **understand** something is to know what it means.
*My cousin Ernest can **understand** French.*

> 1) **grasp** 2) **know** 3) **get**

1) *The pilot tried to **grasp** the meaning of the message from the control tower.*
2) *Tom and Tim **know** how aeroplanes work.*
3) *The new student did not **get** the joke.*

Opposite: **misunderstand**

Bonjour!

undo verb

To **undo** means to loosen or untie.
*Dad wanted to **undo** the parcel quickly.*

> 1) **untie** 2) **open** 3) **unbutton**

1) *I started to **untie** the knots.*
2) *Someone has already **opened** the box.*
3) *The doctor **unbuttoned** his coat.*

Opposites: **fasten, tie**

unfair adjective

If something is **unfair**, it is not right or equal.
*Todd is an **unfair** player who always cheats.*

> 1) **unjust** 2) **biased** 3) **one-sided** 4) **prejudiced**

1) *The prisoner was given an **unjust** sentence.*
2) *The driver wrote a **biased** report about the accident.*
3) *The general gave a **one-sided** account of the enemy's attack.*
4) *Mr Jones has a **prejudiced** view of teenagers.*

unfold verb

To **unfold** means to open up or spread out.
*Mum asked Liam to **unfold** the sheets.*

> 1) **unfurl** 2) **open** 3) **spread out**

1) *The explorers **unfurled** their country's flag.*
2) *Ben couldn't wait to **open** his presents.*
3) *The navigator **spread out** the map to check their position.*

Opposite: **fold**

unhappy adjective

If you are **unhappy**, you feel sad.
*Josh was **unhappy** when his model plane broke.*

> 1) **dismal** 2) **downcast** 3) **miserable** 4) **sad**

1) *Faith was **dismal** after her grandparents left.*
2) *He was **downcast** because he did not make the team.*
3) *The **miserable** woman never seemed to smile.*
4) *The girl was **sad** because her best friend had moved away.*

Opposites: **glad, happy**

unkind adjective

If someone is **unkind**, that person causes
pain and sadness to others.
*It is **unkind** to tease shy people.*

> 1) **cruel** 2) **nasty** 3) **mean** 4) **spiteful**

1) *The **cruel** man left his dog out in the rain.*
2) *"Don't be so **nasty**!" sobbed Helena.*
3) *I don't like it when people are **mean** to me.*
4) *Our neighbour was a **spiteful** person.*

Opposite: **kind**

unknown adjective

If something is **unknown**, it is not part
of someone's knowledge.
*An **unknown** number of poppies grows in this field.*

1) **untold** 2) **unnamed** 3) **anonymous**

1) *There are **untold** treasures buried at sea.*
2) *The actor got a letter from an **unnamed** admirer.*
3) *My favourite poem is by an **anonymous** writer.*

Opposite: **known**

untidy adjective

If something is **untidy**, it is in a mess.
*Cliff was told to straighten up his **untidy** room.*

1) **cluttered** 2) **sloppy** 3) **messy** 3) **chaotic**

1) *Our attic is **cluttered** with old junk.*
2) *The **sloppy** boy was told to get cleaned up.*
3) *Ginny had to explain why her work was **messy**.*
4) *The playroom was **chaotic** after the birthday party.*

Opposites: **neat, tidy**

upset adjective

To be **upset** means to be unhappy because of something
that has happened.
*Lindsay was **upset** when she lost her favourite necklace.*

1) **sad** 2) **dismayed** 3) **troubled**

1) *The film made the young children **sad**.*
2) *We were **dismayed** when our house burned down.*
3) *"I am **troubled** to hear such bad news," said the businessman.*

Opposites: **happy, pleased**

urge   noun

An **urge** is a strong feeling of wanting to do something.
*When I saw Lizzie yawn, I had an **urge** to yawn, too.*

1) **need** 2) **desire** 3) **longing**

1) *The itchy flea bite gave me the **need** to scratch.*
2) *I had a real **desire** to visit my cousin in the Bahamas.*
3) *After waiting for 12 hours, the tired passengers had
    a **longing** for sleep.*

urgent   adjective

Something **urgent** needs attention right away.
*The nurse got an **urgent** message to call the hospital.*

1) **important** 2) **crucial** 3) **pressing**

1) *My parents got an **important** letter from the headteacher.*
2) *It's **crucial** to see a doctor if you think you have appendicitis.*
3) *The executive had to rush because she had a **pressing** appointment.*

use   verb

To **use** something means to put it into action.
*You **use** a pen to write a letter.*

1) **employ** 2) **utilize** 3) **wield**

1) *We **employed** our brains to solve the mystery.*
2) *She **utilized** a mop to clean the floor.*
3) *You **wield** an axe to chop wood.*

Uu useful

useful adjective

If something is **useful**, it helps you or has value.
*Dad bought a **useful** spray attachment for the garden hose.*

> 1) **practical** 2) **handy** 3) **helpful**

1) *An umbrella is **practical** in the rain.*
2) *Dad got some **handy** hints about looking after his car.*
3) *Mum thanked Gilbert for being a **helpful** boy.*

Opposite: **useless**

useless adjective

If something is **useless**, it has no purpose or meaning.
*The hairbrush was **useless** to the bald man.*

> 1) **pointless** 2) **worthless** 3) **futile**

1) *It was **pointless** to keep the broken toys.*
2) *The torch was **worthless** without batteries.*
3) *"It is **futile** to try to escape," said the guard.*

Opposite: **useful**

usual adjective

If something is **usual**, it is normal or typical.
*Dad bought his **usual** newspaper from the shop.*

> 1) **routine** 2) **customary** 3) **regular**

1) *We were asked the **routine** questions.*
2) *The director sat in his **customary** chair.*
3) *Grant went on his **regular** evening walk.*

Opposite: **unusual**

190

vain adjective

If you are **vain**, you think too highly of yourself.
*Betty was **vain** about her appearance.*

1) **conceited** 2) **proud** 3) **self-important**

1) *Brian was **conceited** about his football skills.*
2) *Margaret was **proud** of her long, blonde hair.*
3) *The mayor was a **self-important** man.*

Opposite: **modest**

valuable adjective

If something is **valuable**, it is important or worth lots of money.
*The British crown jewels are very **valuable**.*

1) **costly** 2) **precious** 3) **prized** 4) **treasured**

1) *The **costly** ruby necklace sparkled.*
2) *A rival company stole the **precious** documents.*
3) *Emeralds are highly **prized** jewels.*
4) *My grandfather's watch is my most **treasured** possession.*

Opposite: **worthless**

vanish verb

To **vanish** means to disappear.
*At the end of the show the magician made
the rabbit **vanish**.*

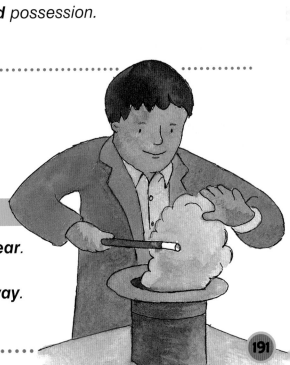

1) **disappear** 2) **evaporate** 3) **fade away**

1) *Wizard William could make anything **disappear**.*
2) *The water **evaporated** in the hot sunshine.*
3) *My face cream made my blemishes **fade away**.*

Opposite: **appear**

vast adjective

Something that is **vast** is extremely big.
*America's prairies cover a **vast** area.*

> 1) **huge** 2) **immense** 3) **enormous** 4) **limitless**

1) *The white rhinoceros has a **huge** horn.*
2) *We saw some **immense** temples in India.*
3) *The university has an **enormous** amount of research money.*
4) *Outer space is **limitless**.*

Opposite: **tiny**

vegetable noun

A **vegetable** is a plant you can eat.
*The farm store sells lots of different **vegetables**.*

broccoli

carrots

sweetcorn

leeks

potatoes

peas

onions

cauliflower

very adverb

Very means to a great degree.
*The winner of the race ran **very** fast.*

> 1) **absolutely** 2) **exceedingly** 3) **extremely** 4) **particularly**

1) *The soprano sang **absolutely** beautifully at the concert.*
2) *My sister works **exceedingly** hard at school.*
3) *Josh was **extremely** lucky to win the prize.*
4) *The editor wrote **particularly** neatly.*

Opposites: **hardly, slightly**

view noun

The **view** is what you can see from
where you are.
*The **view** from the hotel bedroom is lovely.*

> 1) **scene** 2) **vista** 3) **outlook**

1) *The artist painted the mountain **scene**.*
2) *A **vista** of flowers lay in front of us.*
3) *"What a nice **outlook**!" said the guide.*

viewer noun

A **viewer** is someone who watches.
*The TV star was liked by the **viewers**.*

> 1) **watcher** 2) **observer** 3) **spectator** 4) **onlooker**

1) *The bird **watcher** observed the robins through his binoculars.*
2) *The new employee was an **observer** at the important meeting.*
3) *The **spectators** enjoyed the tennis match.*
4) *Several **onlookers** watched as the firefighters tackled the blaze.*

violent adjective

To be **violent** means to use a lot of force or strength.
*The **violent** wind blew the roof off the house.*

> 1) **savage** 2) **fiery** 3) **raging** 4) **brutal**

1) *We wore hats because of the **savage**
   heat of the sun.*
2) *The champion boxer had a **fiery** temper.*
3) *The **raging** ocean pounded the shore.*
4) *The **brutal** tiger attacked its prey.*

Opposites: **calm, gentle, peaceful**

visible adjective

If something is **visible**, it can be seen.
*The rich man's mansion was **visible** in the distance.*

> 1) **noticeable** 2) **clear** 3) **apparent** 4) **in view**

1) *The batsman had a **noticeable** bruise on his arm.*
2) *Babies sometimes have **clear** birthmarks.*
3) *The man's surprise was **apparent** on his face.*
4) *My presents were **in view** on the table.*

Opposite: **invisible**

visit verb

To **visit** means to go to see someone or something.
*Dad took us to **visit** the city zoo.*

> 1) **call on** 2) **go to see** 3) **look up**

1) *"Don't forget to **call on** Grandpa," said Mum.*
2) *We **go to see** our cousins once a year.*
3) *The former student went to **look up** his old friends.*

visit noun

A **visit** is a trip to see someone or a short stay in a place.
Grandma went on a visit to her sister's house.

> 1) **holiday** 2) **trip** 3) **outing**

1) *Our **holiday** at the beach was lots of fun.*
2) *"I am going on a **trip** to Australia," said Vincent.*
3) *The class went on an **outing** to the museum.*

visitor noun

A **visitor** is someone who visits a place or a person.
The visitors were given a guided tour.

> 1) **caller** 2) **company** 3) **guest** 4) **tourist**

1) *They had lots of **callers** when the baby was born.*
2) *"I enjoy having **company**," said Aunt Beatrice.*
3) *The **guests** were given the best rooms.*
4) *Every summer the city is filled with **tourists**.*

vivid adjective

Something that is **vivid** is very strong and colourful.
The artist painted a vivid portrait of my great uncle.

> 1) **brilliant** 2) **bright** 3) **dazzling**

1) *Every year I look forward to seeing the **brilliant** autumn leaves.*
2) *Our new puppy has **bright** green eyes.*
3) *The car's headlights were **dazzling**.*

Opposites: **dull, pale**

wait verb

To **wait** means to stay in one place or do nothing until something happens.
*I **wait** for the school bus on the corner.*

> 1) **linger** 2) **loiter** 3) **remain**

1) *The gardener did not want to **linger** in the cold.*
2) *The lazy boy **loitered** outside the school gate.*
3) *I **remained** at the house until my friends arrived.*

wake verb

To **wake** means to stop being asleep.
*Kevin has to **wake** at seven o'clock.*

> 1) **rise** 2) **rouse** 3) **stir**

1) *Most farmers have to **rise** before dawn.*
2) *The lazy man did not **rouse** until lunchtime.*
3) *Grandpa was so tired he did not **stir** when the alarm clock went off.*

Opposite: **sleep**

walk verb

To **walk** means to move along on foot.
*Jess likes to **walk** to school.*

> 1) **amble** 2) **hike** 3) **stride** 4) **stroll**

1) *My elderly neighbour likes to **amble** to the newsagent every morning.*
2) *The family **hikes** five miles every Sunday.*
3) *My dad **strides** very fast.*
4) *"Let's go for a **stroll**," suggested Theo.*

wander verb

To **wander** means to move around with no purpose.
*The girls **wander** around the shops on Saturday.*

> 1) **roam** 2) **meander** 3) **drift** 4) **rove**

1) *The traveller had **roamed** all over Europe.*
2) *Zack and I **meandered** through the fairground.*
3) *The lonely boy **drifted** around the city centre.*
4) *The hunters **roved** through the forest.*

want verb

To **want** something means to wish to have it.
*She **wants** a new dress for the school dance.*

> 1) **desire** 2) **crave** 3) **long for**

1) *"I **desire** to speak to you," said the teacher.*
2) *The miserable children **craved** some fun.*
3) *The wet campers **longed for** a sunny day.*

warm adjective

If something is **warm**, it is of medium heat.
*The bus driver wears a **warm** coat in the winter.*

> 1) **balmy** 2) **heated** 3) **tepid**

1) *It was such a **balmy** day that we
   decided to sit by the pool.*
2) *The water in the swimming
   pool was **heated**.*
3) *Edna washed her woollen
   sweater in **tepid** water.*

Opposite: **cool**

wash verb

To **wash** something means to clean it with water.
*Dad had to **wash** Sam's football shirt.*

> 1) **bathe** 2) **clean** 3) **launder** 4) **rinse**

1) *I had to **bathe** our smelly dog.*
2) *Dad decided to **clean** the fish tank.*
3) *You can **launder** clothes at
   a laundrette.*
4) *Kendra **rinsed** her muddy hands
   under the tap.*

waste verb

To **waste** something means to use it up carelessly.
*The governor told people not to **waste** water.*

> 1) **throw away** 2) **fritter away** 3) **squander**

1) *The boys **throw away** their money on silly games.*
2) *"Don't **fritter away** your pocket money," said Dad.*
3) *Tamara **squandered** her time at school.*

Opposite: **save**

watch verb

To **watch** something means to look at it.
*"I don't want to **watch** TV," said Samantha.*

> 1) **observe** 2) **view** 3) **stare at** 4) **gaze**

1) *Daniel **observed** the football game.*
2) *We wanted to **view** the race.*
3) *"Don't **stare at** me," said the injured boy.*
4) *I saw a large tanker as I **gazed** out to sea.*

wave   verb

To **wave** means to move from side to side or up and down.
*The flags **wave** in the gentle breeze.*

> 1) **flutter** 2) **flap** 3) **sway**

1) *The sheets **flutter** on the clothesline.*
2) *"Don't **flap** the newspaper around," said Dad.*
3) *The young trees **swayed** in the storm.*

way   noun

A **way** of doing something is a method of doing it.
*There are lots of **ways** to cook eggs.*

> 1) **method** 2) **manner** 3) **fashion**

1) *The children learned a new **method** of tying their shoelaces.*
2) *The saleswoman spoke in a rude **manner**.*
3) *My grandmother writes in an odd **fashion**.*

weak   adjective

Someone or something that is **weak** has very little strength.
*I am strong but my younger brother is **weak**.*

> 1) **feeble** 2) **delicate** 3) **frail** 4) **puny**

1) *The sick man was too **feeble** to get out of bed.*
2) *My brother was **delicate** when he was young.*
3) *The **frail** old man walked with a cane.*
4) *Our dog was **puny** when he was a puppy.*

Opposite: **strong**

weather noun

The **weather** is the state of the air outside.
*In the summer the **weather** can be hot and sunny.*

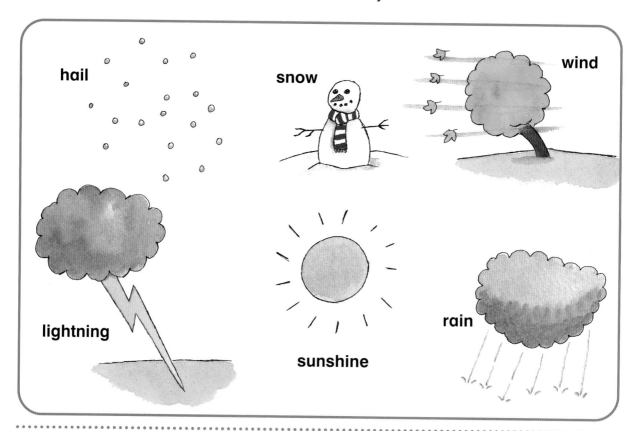

hail

snow

wind

lightning

sunshine

rain

weird adjective

If something is **weird**, it is strange or unusual.
*The artist's house was a **weird** shape.*

1) **strange** 2) **peculiar** 3) **odd** 4) **unusual**

1) *I saw a **strange** picture on the wall.*
2) *The spicy food tasted **peculiar**.*
3) *"You look really **odd**," said my best friend.*
4) *The film star wore **unusual** clothes.*

Opposites: **usual, normal**

welcome adjective

If something is **welcome**, it is received gladly.
*The hotel guest felt very **welcome**.*

> 1) **acceptable** 2) **wanted** 3) **pleasant**

1) *"This is an **acceptable** idea," said Professor Lau.*
2) *Our new kitten is a **wanted** addition to our home.*
3) *I got a **pleasant** surprise in the post today.*

Opposites: **unwanted, unwelcome**

well adjective

If you are **well**, you are healthy.
*The doctor told me I was **well**.*

> 1) **fit** 2) **thriving** 3) **healthy**

1) *Olympic athletes have to be very **fit**.*
2) *"Your dog is **thriving**," said the vet.*
3) *Our local farmer always looks **healthy**.*

Opposites: **ill, sick, unwell**

well adverb

If something is done **well**, it is done in a good way.
*The book on the sights of Rome was **well** written.*

> 1) **agreeably** 2) **acceptably** 3) **properly**

1) *The students promised to behave **agreeably**.*
2) *"You have done your work **acceptably**," said Mr Dixon.*
3) *The tour guide liked to do her job **properly**.*

Opposite: **badly**

Ww wet

wet adjective

To be **wet** means to be covered with liquid.
*Jason hung the **wet** clothes on the line.*

> 1) **moist** 2) **soggy** 3) **soaking** 4) **sopping**

1) *The dog's nose was **moist**.*
2) *I pulled the **soggy** book out of the water.*
3) *"You're **soaking**!" cried Mum when I came in from the rain.*
4) *He put the **sopping** clothes into the dryer.*

Opposite: **dry**

whisper verb

To **whisper** means to speak in a soft voice.
*I was not even allowed to **whisper**.*

> 1) **murmur** 2) **sigh** 3) **hiss**

1) *The assistant **murmured** the answer into his ear.*
2) *The teacher **sighed** my name.*
3) *"Turn the light off!" **hissed** Connie.*

whole adjective

If something is **whole**, it has nothing left out.
*Michael wanted to eat the **whole** apple pie.*

> 1) **entire** 2) **total** 3) **full** 4) **complete**

1) *"I have finished the **entire** book," boasted my sister.*
2) *The cashier wanted the **total** amount.*
3) *I wanted Dad to read the **full** story.*
4) *We spent a **complete** day in silence.*

Opposite: **partial**

wicked adjective

To be **wicked** means to be very bad.
*The **wicked** witch mixed up a potion.*

> 1) **heartless** 2) **fiendish** 3) **evil**

1) *A **heartless** thief stole the old man's life savings.*
2) *The **fiendish** pirate attacked the ship.*
3) *The cruel dictator had an **evil** plan.*

Opposites: **good, harmless**

wide adjective

If something is **wide** it measures a long way from one side to the other.
*The presenter of the new game show wore **wide** trousers.*

> 1) **large** 2) **broad** 3) **vast**

1) *The dog escaped through a **large** gap in the fence.*
2) *The giant had **broad** shoulders.*
3) *The fleet of ships sailed down the **vast** river.*

Opposite: **narrow**

wild adjective

If something is **wild**, it lives freely.
*In the nature reserve we saw lots of **wild** animals.*

> 1) **untamed** 2) **feral** 3) **free**

1) *The **untamed** horse could not be ridden.*
2) *There is a **feral** cat living in the woods.*
3) *I wanted the circus animals to be **free**.*

Opposite: **tame**

win verb

To **win** means to finish first in a game or competition.
*Debbie was pleased to **win** the sack race.*

> 1) **triumph**   2) **come in first**   3) **succeed**

1) *The girls' team **triumphed** in the netball competition.*
2) *Jamie **came in first** in the 100-metre sprint.*
3) *Everyone tried to beat the last year's winner, but he **succeeded**.*

Opposite: **lose**

wind noun

Wind is a current of air.
*The **wind** blew my umbrella inside out.*

> 1) **breeze**   2) **draft**   3) **gust**

1) *A **breeze** made the flowers move.*
2) *The **draft** came in through the window.*
3) *Robbie felt a cold **gust** on his neck.*

wind verb

To **wind** something means to turn or coil it.
*Dad **winds** the hose up after he has used it.*

> 1) **bend**   2) **twist**   3) **curve**

1) *I tried to **bend** the wire around my finger.*
2) *The climber **twisted** the rope around his waist.*
3) *"The road **curves** to the left," said the driver.*

Opposite: **straighten**

winner noun

The **winner** is the person who wins a contest or battle.
*Mum was the **winner** of the chess game.*

> 1) **victor** 2) **champion** 3) **conqueror**

1) *"Three cheers for the **victor**!" cheered the umpire.*
2) *Stephen had run fastest, so he was the **champion**.*
3) *The battle was over, and the prince was the **conqueror**.*

Opposite: **loser**

woods noun

Woods consist of a large group of trees.
*We went for a stroll in the **woods**.*

> 1) **forest** 2) **copse** 3) **grove**

1) *"I found some acorns in the **forest**," said Nat.*
2) *The **copse** is our favourite place.*
3) *Big apple trees grow in the **grove**.*

work noun

Work is physical or mental effort.
*The delivery man had lots of **work** to do.*

> 1) **labour** 2) **toil** 3) **effort**

1) *Building houses is hard **labour**.*
2) *Ruben's **toil** was rewarded with praise.*
3) *The **effort** made her very tired.*

Opposites: **play, rest**

worry verb

To **worry** means to feel concerned.
We all started to worry about the weather.

> 1) **fret** 2) **agonize** 3) **be anxious**

1) *We tried not to fret about the missing costumes.*
2) *I agonized about the terrible secret of my missing brother.*
3) *"Try not to be so anxious," said the kind nurse.*

write verb

To **write** means to form words with a pen or pencil, or to create something with words.
The English students had to write a story.

> 1) **compose** 2) **jot down** 3) **scribble**

1) *Daryl tried to compose a thank-you letter.*
2) *Mum said she would jot down a shopping list.*
3) *We had to scribble some notes in our notebooks.*

wrong adjective

If something is **wrong** it is not correct.
The dancer put on the wrong shoes.

> 1) **mistaken** 2) **in error** 3) **incorrect**

1) *The cashier said that he had been mistaken.*
2) *"I think you are in error," said Uncle Pete.*
3) *I gave an incorrect answer in our class quiz.*

Opposites: **correct, right**

yell verb

To **yell** means to shout loudly.

*Her little brother **yells** if he doesn't get what he wants.*

> 1) **bawl** 2) **bellow** 3) **scream** 4) **screech**

1) *Babies **bawl** loudly if they get upset.*
2) *The teacher **bellowed** at the noisy children.*
3) *Some people **scream** if you scare them.*
4) *"Do as you are told!" **screeched** the coach.*

Opposite: **whisper**

young adjective

If you are **young** you have only been alive for a short time.

*A kitten is a **young** cat.*

A young person
is a baby.

A young cow
is a calf.

A young hen
is a chick.

A young horse
is a foal.

A young dog
is a puppy.

A young duck
is a duckling.

Zz zero

zero noun

Zero is nothing at all.
*Dan got **zero** in his science test.*

> 1) **nothing** 2) **blank** 3) **naught**

1) *The final score for each team was **nothing**.*
2) *There was a **blank** space on the form.*
3) *His holiday plans came to **naught**.*

zone noun

A **zone** is a place that has a special use.
*We sat in the non-smoking **zone** of the airport.*

> 1) **area** 2) **region** 3) **section**

1) *We parked our car in the blue **area** of the car park.*
2) *She lives in the wine-making **region** of Italy.*
3) *The food **section** of the store was closed.*

zoom verb

To **zoom** is to move very quickly.
*The jet plane **zoomed** overhead.*

> 1) **dart** 2) **dash** 3) **speed**

1) *The dragonfly **darted** across the pond.*
2) *I **dashed** inside when I heard the phone ring.*
3) *The driver tried to **speed** around the track in record time.*

Index

All the headwords and synonyms that appear in the thesaurus are listed in alphabetical order in this index.

When you find a word in the alphabetical list, the headword entry you need to look up is given after the word *see*. For some words, there is more than one headword to look up, for example **admire**.

Where a word or headword is listed more than once, to help you find the right word the different meanings or the parts of speech are given in brackets afterwards: for example, **bad** (naughty) and **bad** (rotten) or **end** (noun) and **end** (verb).

Index

available *see* FREE
average *see* NORMAL
avid *see* KEEN
avoid *see* MISS
awake *see* AWAKE
away *see* ABSENT, OUT
awful *see* AWFUL, HORRIBLE

B

baby *see* BABY, CHILD, KID
backside *see* BOTTOM
bad (naughty) *see* AWFUL, BAD,
 EVIL, NAUGHTY
bad (rotten) *see* BAD
bad-mannered *see* RUDE
bake *see* BAKE
balance *see* REST (noun)
balmy *see* WARM
band (group) *see* BAND
band (ring) *see* BAND
bang *see* KNOCK, THUD
banquet *see* MEAL
bare *see* BARE, EMPTY
base *see* BOTTOM
bashful *see* SHY
bathe *see* WASH
batter *see* HIT
battle *see* FIGHT
bawl *see* SHOUT, YELL
be anxious *see* WORRY
be concerned *see* CARE
be fond of *see* LIKE (verb)
be recumbent *see* LIE
be sure of *see* KNOW
beam *see* SHINE
beast *see* BEAST, CREATURE
beautiful *see* BEAUTIFUL, LOVELY,
 PRETTY
bed *see* BOTTOM
begin *see* START
behave *see* BEHAVE
behind *see* BOTTOM, LATE
being *see* CREATURE
belated *see* LATE
believe *see* TRUST
bellow *see* SHOUT, YELL
below *see* UNDER
bend (noun) *see* BEND (noun)
bend (verb) *see* BEND (verb),
 KNEEL, WIND (verb)
beneath *see* UNDER
beside *see* NEAR
better *see* BETTER

between *see* BETWEEN
biased *see* UNFAIR
bicker *see* ARGUE
big *see* BIG, GREAT, LARGE, TALL
bind *see* KNOT
bird *see* BIRD
bit *see* BIT, PIECE
bizarre *see* EXTRAORDINARY,
 ODD
blank *see* NOTHING, ZERO
blaring *see* LOUD
blaze *see* BURN
blend *see* MIX
blissful *see* HAPPY
blow *see* SURPRISE
blue *see* SAD
blunder *see* MISTAKE
boast *see* BOAST
boastful *see* PROUD
boat *see* BOAT
boisterous *see* EXCITED
bold *see* BRAVE
bombshell *see* SURPRISE
bonus *see* GIFT
boring *see* BORING, DULL
bother *see* ANNOY
bottom (backside) *see* BOTTOM
bottom (base) *see* BOTTOM
bounce *see* JUMP
bow down *see* KNEEL
brag *see* BOAST
brain *see* MIND
brainless *see* STUPID
brainy *see* BRIGHT
brand *see* SORT
brave *see* BRAVE
brawl *see* FIGHT
brawny *see* TOUGH
break (noun) *see* BREAK (noun),
 REST
break (verb) *see* BREAK (verb)
breed *see* KIND (noun)
breeze *see* WIND (noun)
bright (brainy) *see* BRIGHT
bright (shiny) *see* BRIGHT, VIVID
brilliant *see* BRIGHT, VIVID
bring *see* BRING, DRAW
brisk *see* QUICK
broad *see* THICK, WIDE
brood *see* SULK
bruise *see* HURT
brutal *see* CRUEL, VIOLENT
build *see* BUILD, MAKE
building *see* BUILDING

bulky *see* HEAVY
bumpy *see* ROUGH
burn *see* BURN
burning *see* HOT
burrow *see* DIG
bury *see* BURY
bustling *see* BUSY
busy *see* BUSY
bum *see* BOTTOM

C

calamity *see* DISASTER
calculate *see* COUNT
call (announce) *see* CALL
call (visit) *see* CALL
call on *see* INVITE, VISIT (verb)
call to mind *see* REMEMBER
caller *see* VISITOR
calm *see* CALM, PATIENT
calm down *see* RELAX
capable *see* ABLE
capture *see* CATCH, TRAP
care *see* CARE
careless *see* CARELESS, LAZY
carry *see* BRING, CARRY, HOLD,
 MOVE
carry out *see* DO
carve *see* CUT
cash *see* MONEY
catastrophe *see* DISASTER
catch *see* CATCH, TRAP
cease *see* END (verb), STOP
celebrated *see* FAMOUS
centre *see* MIDDLE
certain *see* CERTAIN, SURE
chain *see* ROW
champion *see* WINNER
chance *see* RISK
change *see* CHANGE, MONEY
changed *see* DIFFERENT
chaos *see* MESS
chaotic *see* UNTIDY
charge *see* ORDER
charitable *see* GENEROUS
charming *see* BEAUTIFUL, NICE
chase *see* CHASE, FOLLOW
chat *see* CHAT, SPEAK, TALK
cheap *see* CHEAP
cheat *see* TRICK
check *see* CHECK
chew *see* EAT
chief *see* MAIN
child *see* BABY, CHILD, KID

Index

Index

Index

interesting *see* INTERESTING
interior *see* INSIDE
intermission *see* BREAK (noun)
internal *see* INSIDE
interrogate *see* ASK, QUESTION
intriguing *see* INTERESTING
invisible *see* INVISIBLE
invite *see* INVITE
irate *see* MAD
irritate *see* ANNOY
irritated *see* CROSS
irritation *see* NUISANCE
isolated *see* LONELY
issue *see* MATTER, TOPIC
item *see* OBJECT, THING

 J

jealous *see* JEALOUS
jerk *see* JOLT
jest *see* JOKE (noun)
jet *see* JET
jewel *see* JEWEL
job *see* JOB
join *see* JOIN
joke (noun) *see* JOKE (noun)
joke (verb) *see* JOKE (verb)
jolt *see* JOLT, SURPRISE
jostle *see* JOLT
jot down *see* WRITE
journey *see* JOURNEY
joyful *see* GLAD
judge (noun) *see* JUDGE (noun)
judge (verb) *see* JUDGE (verb)
jumble *see* MESS
jump *see* JUMP
just *see* FAIR, ONLY (adv)

K

keen *see* EAGER, KEEN, SHARP
keep *see* KEEP, SAVE
key *see* IMPORTANT
kid *see* KID
kill *see* KILL
killed *see* DEAD
kind (adj) *see* KIND (adj)
kind (noun) *see* KIND (noun),
SORT
kneel *see* KNEEL
knock *see* KNOCK
knock down *see* DESTROY
knot *see* KNOT
know (identify) *see* KNOW

know (realize) *see* KNOW,
UNDERSTAND
knowledge *see* KNOWLEDGE

 L

labour *see* WORK
land (noun) *see* LAND (noun)
land (verb) *see* LAND (verb)
lanky *see* TALL
large *see* BIG, LARGE, WIDE
last (adj) *see* LAST (adj)
last (verb) *see* LAST (verb)
late *see* LATE
later *see* NEXT
latest *see* MODERN
laugh *see* LAUGH
launder *see* WASH
lavish *see* GENEROUS
law *see* RULE (noun)
lay *see* PLACE (verb)
layer *see* LAYER
laze *see* RELAX
lazy *see* LAZY, SLOW
lead *see* GUIDE, LEAD, RULE
(verb)
leading *see* IMPORTANT
lean *see* THIN
leap *see* JUMP
leave *see* LEAVE, GO (verb)
leftover *see* SPARE
legend *see* STORY
leisure activity *see* HOBBY
leisurely *see* SLOW
lengthy *see* LONG (adj)
level *see* EVEN
liberal *see* GENEROUS
lie *see* LIE
lifeless *see* DEAD
lift *see* RAISE
light (adj) *see* LIGHT (adj)
light (noun) *see* LIGHT (noun)
lightweight *see* LIGHT (adj)
like (adj) *see* LIKE (adj)
like (verb) *see* ENJOY, LIKE (verb)
limitless *see* VAST
line *see* ROW
linger *see* STAY, WAIT
link *see* JOIN
litter *see* LITTER, RUBBISH
little *see* LITTLE, SHORT, SMALL,
TINY
lively *see* ACTIVE, EXCITED
load *see* FILL

loathe *see* DISLIKE, HATE
location *see* PLACE (noun)
lock *see* CLOSE
lofty *see* HIGH
loiter *see* WAIT
lone *see* ONLY (adj)
lonely *see* LONELY
long (adj) *see* LONG (adj)
long (verb) *see* LONG (verb)
long for *see* MISS, WANT
long-faced *see* SERIOUS
long-suffering *see* PATIENT
longing *see* URGE
look *see* LOOK
look over *see* CHECK
look up *see* VISIT (verb)
loom *see* APPEAR
loop *see* KNOT
lose *see* LOSE
lost *see* EXTINCT
loud *see* LOUD, NOISY
lounge *see* LIE
love *see* ENJOY, LOVE
lovely *see* BEAUTIFUL, LOVELY,
PRETTY
loving *see* KIND (adj)

 M

machine *see* MACHINE
mad *see* MAD
magic *see* MAGIC
magnanimous *see* GENEROUS
mail *see* SEND
main *see* MAIN
majestic *see* GRAND
make (compel) *see* MAKE
make (create) *see* BUILD, COOK,
MAKE
make clear *see* EXPLAIN
make tracks *see* LEAVE
manner *see* WAY
many *see* MANY
march *see* MARCH
mark *see* MARK
mash *see* CRUSH
massive *see* ENORMOUS, LARGE
match *see* MATCH
matching *see* SAME
matter *see* MATTER
mature *see* ADULT
meal *see* MEAL
mean (adj) *see* MEAN (adj),
UNKIND

215

Index

part *see* PART
particularly *see* VERY
pass (give) *see* PASS
pass (go by) *see* PASS
pastime *see* HOBBY
pat *see* TOUCH
patch *see* FIX
patient *see* PATIENT
pause *see* BREAK (noun)
peaceful *see* CALM, PEACEFUL
peak *see* TOP
peculiar *see* FUNNY, ODD, STRANGE, WEIRD
penniless *see* POOR
perfect *see* IDEAL, PERFECT
perform *see* DO
performer *see* ACTOR
peril *see* DANGER
permission *see* PERMISSION
persist *see* LAST (verb)
pest *see* NUISANCE
pester *see* ANNOY
pet *see* FEEL, PET
pick *see* CHOOSE, PICK
piece *see* BIT, PART, PIECE
piercing *see* NOISY
pile *see* PILE
pine *see* MISS
pitch *see* THROW
pivot *see* TURN
place (noun) *see* PLACE (noun)
place (verb) *see* PLACE (verb)
plain *see* CLEAR, EASY, SIMPLE
plan *see* ARRANGE, IDEA
planet *see* PLANET
plant *see* PLANT
play *see* PLAY
player *see* ACTOR
pleasant *see* MILD, NICE, WELCOME
please *see* PLEASE
pleased *see* GLAD, PROUD
plodding *see* SLOW
pluck *see* GRAB
plucky *see* BRAVE
plump *see* FAT
plunge *see* DIVE, FALL
pointless *see* USELESS
pointy *see* SHARP
polished *see* SMOOTH
polite *see* GOOD
ponder *see* THINK
poor *see* POOR
portion *see* PART

position *see* PLACE (noun)
positive *see* CERTAIN, SURE
possess *see* HAVE
poster *see* NOTICE (noun)
practical *see* SENSIBLE, USEFUL
praise *see* ADMIRE
prank *see* JOKE (noun)
precious *see* VALUABLE
precious stone *see* JEWEL
precise *see* CORRECT, RIGHT
prejudiced *see* UNFAIR
prepare *see* ARRANGE, COOK
prepared *see* READY
present *see* GIFT, GIVE, SHOW
press *see* PUSH
pressing *see* URGENT
pretty *see* PRETTY
previous *see* OLD
previously *see* ONCE
prime *see* MAIN
primed *see* READY
principal *see* MAIN
private *see* SECRET
prized *see* VALUABLE
problem *see* PROBLEM
produce *see* MAKE
professor *see* TEACHER
proper *see* FAIR, PROPER
properly *see* WELL (adv)
protect *see* PROTECT
protected *see* SAFE
proud *see* PROUD, VAIN
provide *see* GIVE
prying *see* NOSY
pull *see* PULL
pull in *see* DRAW
punch *see* HIT
puny *see* WEAK
pure *see* CLEAR
purpose *see* OBJECT
pursue *see* CHASE, FOLLOW
push *see* MOVE, PUSH
put *see* PLACE (verb)
puzzle *see* MYSTERY

Q

quarrel *see* ARGUE, QUARREL
queasy *see* ILL
query *see* ASK
quest *see* QUEST
question *see* DOUBT, QUESTION
quick *see* FAST, QUICK, SUDDEN
quick-witted *see* CLEVER

quiet *see* CALM, PEACEFUL, QUIET, SILENT
quite *see* QUITE
quiver *see* SHAKE
quiz *see* QUESTION

R

race *see* SPEED
radiance *see* GLOW
rage *see* TEMPER
raging *see* MAD, VIOLENT
rain *see* RAIN
raise *see* RAISE
rap *see* KNOCK
rapid *see* FAST, QUICK
ravenous *see* HUNGRY
reach *see* COME
ready *see* READY
real *see* REAL, TRUE
realize *see* KNOW
rear *see* BOTTOM
reason *see* THINK
reasonable *see* CHEAP, SENSIBLE
recall *see* REMEMBER
receive *see* GET
recline *see* LIE
recognize *see* KNOW
recollect *see* REMEMBER
recovered *see* BETTER
reduced *see* CHEAP
referee *see* JUDGE (noun)
refuse *see* REFUSE
region *see* ZONE
regretful *see* SORRY
regular *see* NORMAL, ORDINARY, USUAL
regulation *see* RULE (noun)
relax *see* RELAX
relieved *see* THANKFUL
remain *see* STAY, WAIT
remainder *see* REST
remark *see* SAY
remember *see* KNOW, REMEMBER
remorseful *see* SORRY
remote *see* FARAWAY
repair *see* FIX, MEND
repeatedly *see* OFTEN
reply *see* ANSWER
reptile *see* REPTILE
request *see* ASK
require *see* NEED
rescue *see* RESCUE
resentful *see* JEALOUS

Index

Index